SECOND EDITION

TAKE CHARGE PRODUCT MANAGEMENT

TIME-TESTED TIPS, TACTICS, AND TOOLS FOR
THE NEW OR IMPROVED PRODUCT MANAGER

GREG GERACIE

Actuation Press
CHICAGO, ILLINOIS

Greg Geracie/Actuation Press

ISBN: 978-0-9831116-3-4
Library of Congress Control Number: 2016906084

Product management
Product management — Handbooks, manuals, etc.
New products — Management
Marketing

Cover design and illustrations by Kathleen Riley.

Ordering Information: Quantity sales. Special discounts are available on quantity purchases by corporations, associations, and others. Contact the author at www.ActuationConsulting.com

Take Charge Product Management — Second Edition: June, 2016

CONTENTS

THERE HAS NEVER BEEN ANOTHER PRODUCT MANAGEMENT BOOK LIKE THIS.

Take Charge Product Management actually takes you inside the role of a product manager and provides a clearly defined path to success. It lays out an innovative approach that uniquely recognizes that the size of your company matters, and helps you understand how size — and your company's business objectives — impact your role. You will be able to use the tips, tactics, and tools in this book to successfully grow your products and take charge of your career!

"*Take Charge Product Management* is a great read to understand both the field and the role of product management. However this book goes further with valuable lessons for all product managers to master including; product lifecycle management, aligning development and product management goals, and establishing process around business outcomes. It's a truly enjoyable read."

– Greg Cohen, author of *Agile Excellence for Product Managers*

"Geracie nails it with *Take Charge Product Management*. This book is a comprehensive guide to becoming a highly effective product manager. The book's format really brings home the tools and processes that are required to become a leader in any organization's product management function. *Take Charge Product Management* should be the new bible for all product managers."

– Kevin Maguire, General Manager, Philips Healthcare

"Greg Geracie has compiled a thoroughly "user friendly', 232-page compendium of instructions, advice, commentary, insights, tips, tricks, tools and techniques for adding value...a complete course under one cover! "Take Charge" fully lives up to the promise of its title and is enthusiastically recommended reading!"

– The Midwest Book Review

"I wish I had this book 10 years ago when I had started my career...but what is nice about this book is that I know I will continue to use it for the next 10 years of my career."

– Silicon Valley Product Management Association Book Review

"Geracie is teaching through a fundamental tool that all product managers should know, "the user persona/user story". If only text books were written like this, learning would be easier, more relevant, and much more enjoyable."

    – Boston Product Management Association Book Review

"Geracie's *Take Charge Product Management* provides a quick summary of job expectations for new product managers. Written in an accessible manner, the book walks you through a day in the life of a hypothetical product manager, introducing you to challenges product managers face as they enter their roles for the first time."

    – Linda Gorchels, author of *The Product Manager's Handbook and The Product Manager's Field Guide*

"Greg Geracie's book *Take Charge Product Management* does an excellent job of explaining why the role of a product manager is so central to the successful integration of a company's business functions. I also found Greg's description of the Agile software development process and its impact upon product managers to be particularly insightful."

    – MIT Professor Steven Eppinger Co-editor of *The Product Management and Marketing Body of Knowledge*

"*Take Charge Product Management* is a great, easy-to-read book that includes a lot of good tips and nuggets of wisdom about how to operate effectively within an organization as a product manager."

    – Jeff Lash, How To Be A Good Product Manager

"*Take Charge Product Management* is easy to read with a nice casual style to the writing. It's clear that Greg has lived through much (if not all) of Sean's experiences himself during his career and is now imparting the wisdom gained to the next generation of new Product Managers."

    – Saeed Khan, On Product Management

FROM THE AUTHOR

One of the best aspects of writing a book is being able to tell a story from the perspective of the way things should work. This book follows the exploits of Sean Knight, a fictional product manager who works at a fictional company called Alpha Technology Ventures. I based Sean's evolution throughout the book on my observations over the years, learning what does and doesn't work in product management. Many of these insights have come through my own trial and error and ultimately from leading others who shared my passion for the field.

Product management is a function that few, if any, individuals ever trained in until they found themselves in the position. I've written this book to help anyone who finds themselves in a similar position, regardless of whether they just came out of college or, like my friend, Sean, have been a top-achieving professional for years.

CHAPTER ONE: YOUR MISSION, SHOULD YOU CHOOSE TO ACCEPT IT...

The sound of the applause was still ringing in my ears.

Sinclair Jones, Chief Executive Officer (CEO) of Alpha Technology Ventures, had just concluded his speech in honor of our second successful year as a company. The entire team was taking a moment to savor our anniversary. As the din quieted, I thought about the news. Overall, the company was doing well. We just released our first product, and the preliminary feedback was positive. The company was growing rapidly with new team members in sales, marketing, operations, finance, and engineering. We were finally starting to generate some momentum.

However, all was not well behind the scenes. The problem? Every one of our early sales had come with a different set of promises about what the product would do for the client. It was not the sales team's fault as we were lacking a definitive value proposition. To make matters worse, the engineering team was having difficulty prioritizing because each sales person had a different request from their respective clients.

The customer service team was asking us to change aspects of the initial product to accommodate new customers' needs without dropping the ball. Customer service was also increasingly worried that the sales organization's requests were being prioritized above their needs. The facts supported their point of view — our very first customer had left a week earlier, citing lack of customer support.

All of this had taken place in meetings earlier that day, prior to my one-on-one meeting with Sinclair and *before* the celebration. As a member of the sales team, I had become the go-to guy for demonstrating our new product. Everyone was asking for my support because I had an intuitive understanding of what it could do for customers, and I never overcommitted. In fact, Sinclair had asked me to go with him on several customer calls for this very reason. Sinclair explained in our one-on-one meeting that he was going to create a new function in the business: product management. And he asked me to take on the role! I still can't get his question out of my head, "So Sean, can I count on you?" To be honest, I had been so caught off guard that I agreed without even thinking about the ramifications of my decision. But as soon as I left the meeting, the weight of my decision hit me full force. I must have been crazy.

What did I know about product management?

PRODUCT DEFINED

Products are things that satisfy a customer's need or desire. Products generally fall into two broad categories: **tangible and intangible**.

Tangible products are those that you can pick up, touch, and hold. All of the products in a supermarket, from a can of green beans to a frozen turkey, are tangible products. Tangible products exist everywhere and come in all shapes and sizes. The amount of tangible products available is seemingly endless; products are designed to address the needs of customers, and these needs are wide ranging.

Intangible products, on the other hand, are also widely available but cannot be picked up, touched, or held. Examples include services, insurance, business consulting, or training. Like tangible products, intangible products come in a wide variety of forms to address customer needs or desires.

Although the two categories are separate and distinct, product managers often combine them to address specific customer needs and present a more complete solution than either individual type of product would do on its own. When you bought your most recent computer, you likely had a one-year service contract included. Your purchase included a tangible product, the computer, and an intangible product, the one-year service contract. The manufacturer combines both elements to reassure you that they stand behind their product and are willing to address any problems that occur the first year after the sale. Packing these two product types together is often referred to as **bundling**.

MINTING PRODUCT MANAGERS

Newly minted product managers are born every day and are sourced from almost every function. It happens all the time. Why? Because businesses need to manage their growing product lines' complexity while nurturing their revenue streams and profitability. Product managers come from nearly every area of the company because CEOs, like Sinclair, initially look for someone who knows how to work well with customers and who thoroughly understands the product.

These qualities are valued regardless of whether the company is a small, entrepreneurial start-up, a thriving mid-sized company, or a mature and successful multi-billion dollar organization. So let's take a minute and talk about the role that company size and the CEO's level of involvement with the product play in the formation of product management.

ALL STAGES OF COMPANY GROWTH CREATE PRODUCT MANAGER OPPORTUNITIES

In small start-up companies, the CEO often spends a great deal of time and energy developing the company's initial product. This includes identifying a market opportunity, forming a team to pursue the opportunity (which may or may not include a product manager), and building out a preliminary version of the product to show to customers. It also involves initiating a plan to bring the future product to potential clients. Companies like these are small and generally have limited resources. As a result, the CEO is very hands-on, often making most the decisions and actively engaging with clients. Therefore, in many cases the CEO is the product manager. It is not uncommon to find that the CEO of a start-up company was a product manager earlier in their career.

As companies mature, the CEO's role changes as well. Like Sinclair Jones at Alpha Technology Ventures, companies on the verge of leaving the small start-up phase and becoming mid-sized enterprises require the CEO to shift focus. Although the product or products are still critically important to the CEO, other activities like raising financing, scaling the company, growing the customer base, and managing the board of directors take up more of their time. However, as we could see at Alpha Technology Ventures, the singular attention products need does not diminish — it actually increases! So, like Sinclair, executives at this stage of growth create a new function to give more attention to the life blood of the company: products and their revenues.

In more mature companies, the product management function is well established and product managers thrive. As a product manager, you're responsible for product lines that bring in millions in revenue. The CEO is now generally much further removed from the day-to-day operations of the product, but is likely keeping a watchful eye on the trend lines, investments, costs, and the overall health of the company's portfolio of products. The CEO is often actively involved in promoting the company's offerings as well — think Steve Jobs at Apple! However, the need for strong product managers is more important than ever because they vitally contribute to the organization's financial health. In more mature companies, product managers have significantly more resources available to them to manage product lines than they did in either of the two earlier stages of company growth.

At every stage of growth, opportunities abound for product managers to contribute to the success of the enterprise. But as we will see later, the size of the company has a direct bearing on your role as a product manager.

START-UP, MID-SIZED, AND MATURE COMPANIES

A **start-up** is a newly created company looking to introduce innovative products or services that either improve the status quo or create a breakthrough that doesn't already exist. The small team is usually founder-driven, resource-constrained, and constantly iterating until they find clients for the products or services they offer.

A **mid-sized** company has exited the start-up phase and is generating revenue from a small but rapidly expanding base of customers. The company may or may not be founder-driven. The company is quickly becoming an accepted player in the market and is steadily increasing the number of employees needed to scale the business. The focus is on rapid growth.

A **mature** company is established and has an entrenched market position and broad market acceptance. It generates significant revenue from one or more product lines and has a large employee base. Mature companies tend to focus on sustainable growth through both organic growth and mergers and acquisitions.

WHAT EXACTLY IS PRODUCT MANAGEMENT?

That is the million dollar question. The truth is that the roles and responsibilities of product managers vary greatly by industry and company size. In fact, unlike other functional areas, there is greater variability in the scope of responsibilities in your role as a product manager than in other functional areas of your company. For example, sales organizations often follow popular and well-documented methodologies and frameworks as do project management teams. This also holds true for other functional areas of the business.

Don't let the lack of a consistent industry standard scare you. There are many commonalities across all company sizes and types of industries. In fact, the lack of a single consistent standard is your opportunity to imprint your organization and demonstrate the leadership your CEO is counting on. So take a deep breath. Now, let's examine a simple definition of product management.

WHAT'S THE DIFFERENCE BETWEEN STRATEGY AND TACTICS?

The terms **strategy** and **tactics** are often confused. **Strategy** is a carefully crafted and detailed plan of action designed to achieve a specific goal or objective. A strategy explains how a goal is to be achieved.

Tactics, on the other hand, are the actual means used to achieve a specific outcome contributing to a successful strategy.

A strategy is different from a tactic in that different tactics may be deployed as part of a single strategy. For example, one strategy to gain market share would be distributing your product through partners. As part of a company's distribution strategy, you might adopt different tactics like using retail stores, online markets, or wholesalers.

At its most basic, product management is the function responsible for the strategic planning and tactical execution of a company's new and existing products. This includes overseeing all the activities and functions associated with a particular product or family of products.

Product managers act as the field generals for their product, coordinating activities across the diverse functional areas of a business to ensure a maximum return on product investment. Your colleagues will expect you to be the central hub of knowledge about your product for the entire company. You will also be expected to know a great deal about the customers that make up your market and the companies that your organization competes against. Your knowledge will help you chart the course for your product. Charting the course requires you to create a vision for where your product needs to go to stay relevant and profitable and create actionable plans to achieve your company's strategic and financial objectives. At this point you may feel as overwhelmed, regarding the expectations your colleagues have set for you, as Sean did when Sinclair appointed him product manager. However, you may find it reassuring to know that you're not alone. In fact, you'll be able to draw on the support of many people within your organization who share similar goals in achieving market success. As you step into your new role, you'll likely spend a great deal of time interacting with research and development, sales, marketing, operations, legal, finance, and the senior executives at your company as you embark on this career path.

Additionally, I designed the information, tools, and techniques presented in this book to give you a roadmap to market success. A product manager's job is both demanding and fulfilling. To be successful, you'll need a great deal of dedication and self-control. For many product managers, the ability to interact with important customers and chart the course for a successful line of products or services is the most rewarding aspect of their job. Your ability to interact with customers and shepherd your company's products will prove deeply gratifying on both a company and personal level. Market successes will also springboard you to greater levels of responsibility as your career progresses.

ABOUT THIS BOOK

We will be focusing on the information, tools, and techniques of product management throughout this book. My objective is to provide you with a well-defined path as you embark on your career as a product manager. It is important that we take a moment and also discuss some of the assumptions that are built into the book. First, the book assumes that, like most product managers, you did not have training before you assumed your role — just like Sean at Alpha Technology Ventures. However, the scope of this book provides a framework for both newly minted product managers, as well as more seasoned product managers. Second, since the science of product management is highly variable because of the range of industries it crosses and the availability of resources accompanying each company's stage of growth, this book focuses on the common threads rather than highlighting the differences.

Although this book was designed specifically to help product managers succeed within their organizations, the information should also prove helpful to functional business leaders and senior executives. Given that product management lacks a central industry standard, organizations looking to establish a product management function often lack clarity on what product management means, the value of the role, and its boundaries.

Whether you're a CEO looking to implement a product management function or a functional business leader looking to ensure a strong working relationship with a new product management team, the substance of the book should help clarify how the pieces fit.

CHAPTER ONE'S TIPS FOR TAKING CHARGE

- Newly minted product managers can come from virtually any function within an organization. Regardless of your starting point, what matters is that you're committed to understanding the needs of customers and translating those needs into market opportunities for your company.

- As a product manager, your colleagues will expect you to be the field general and subject matter expert for your product or family of products. They will be looking to you to answer a variety of questions about the market, competitors, clients, and prospects. They'll expect you to explain the direction in which you are taking the product.

- A product manager's ability to work collaboratively with other functional areas of the business greatly expands your ability to understand how all the pieces of the business fit together. It also often leads to greater career opportunities as you steer your products to market success.

- The job of the product manager is a demanding one and requires dedication, calm in the face of crises, and the ability to chart a strategic course and execute at a tactical level.

CHAPTER TWO: THE ROLE OF A PRODUCT MANAGER

It was 6:45 a.m. The sharp sound of the alarm clock buzzer cut through my thoughts. Two days had passed since my one-on-one meeting with Sinclair. I'd left the office on Friday grateful for a weekend to contemplate my new opportunity.

Being out of the office gave me time to reflect on the upcoming challenge and all that had happened. As I milled the conversation with Sinclair over and over again in my head, I felt a mix of pride and anxiety.

I hadn't been sleeping when the buzzer rang. I was thinking about what today would bring; it was my first day as a product manager. The one thing I did know came from an email I had read late Sunday afternoon. It was from Sinclair, to me and Linda Welsh, Alpha Technology Ventures Vice President of Human Resources. The email read:

✉ Reply ✉ Reply All ✉ Forward

Sinclair Jones | Linda Welsh; Sean Knight

Product Management Job Description & Organizational Announcement   ∨

Linda and Sean,
We need to quickly put into place a job description for Sean's new position as product manager.
I discussed Sean's role change with Robert, our Vice President of Sales, and he agrees this
change makes sense. Linda, I know you were working to pull together a draft job description.
Please include Sean and get this done before end of day Monday. I want to put out an organizational announcement Tuesday. I'm planning to reach out to the board members over the next
24 hours to let them know about this change before next week's off-site board meeting. Stop by
when it's complete.

Thanks,
Sinclair

After a quick shower, and an even quicker breakfast, I headed into the office for what was sure to be an important day. When I reached my desk I saw that Linda had already arrived and left a Post-it note asking me to stop by as soon as possible regarding Sinclair's email. After a quick stop for coffee, I made my way to Linda's office. After all, understanding what my new job was all about was more important to me than virtually anyone else!

I reached Linda's office and knocked. After several seconds that felt like an eternity, Linda replied "Come in." "Hi Linda, it's me...Sean" I said, my voice cracking slightly as I opened her door. "I saw your Post-it note and the email from Sinclair." Gathering myself, I asked, "Is this a good time to chat?" With a big smile, Linda said, "I don't think your timing could be better Sean." Linda got up and softly closed the door while I sat down at the small table in her office. As Linda walked across the room to join me, I nervously glanced at her screen saver — its message of the day sagely pronounced "when one door closes, another one opens."

That was when I first learned what was going to be expected of me as a product manager...

YOUR RESPONSIBILITIES AS A PRODUCT MANAGER

As Sean is about to learn, one of the best aspects of a product manager's job is the range of activities for which you are responsible. Much will be expected of you, but the sheer variety of activity ensures you'll always be challenged to grow and contribute in new ways to your organization's success.

As a product manager, you're accountable for the overall success or failure of the products you represent. There are many aspects of this responsibility. First, you'll be expected to create a vision for your products. In other words, to envision how your products will not only be successful today, but how they will continue to grow revenue, profitability, and market share over time. To ensure your products' success, now and in the future, you'll be expected to be their primary evangelist both inside your organization and out in the market. You'll be the critical lens that identifies and champions customer needs and translates those needs into actionable plans that grow your product in a way that differentiates your organization from your competitors.

Your role as product manager is to see the forest, not the trees. Your colleagues will expect you to identify and continually monitor market trends. You'll need to conduct or direct market research efforts and analysis on competitors to supplement your existing knowledge.

Your intimate knowledge of the market, customers, competitors, and trends will help you develop a plan of action detailing where you believe your products need to go. It will also enable you to map out a successful path to get there. Once you've mapped out your plan, executives within your organization will likely encourage you to financially justify it with a business case that outlines what the organization can expect in return for investing in it.

SEE THE FOREST, NOT JUST THE TREES

With all the things that are expected of you in your role, it's easy to lose sight of the single most important aspect of your job: maintaining a strategic view of the market you serve. Each function within your organization sees the market from a different perspective, and each unique vantage point is a valuable source of information. However, regardless of the source, there are risks in relying too heavily on any single point of view or customer interaction and extrapolating a market trend. Remember, one customer and their needs, no matter how vocal, does not necessarily indicate a market need. Your job is to remain objective and build a composite view from a variety of angles. This approach allows you to triangulate in on the market opportunities that provide the best chance to attain or maintain a market leadership position and meet your organization's financial objectives.

With a solid business case in hand, you'll be expected to plan, organize, and control products from concept to retirement. To do this, you'll have to work closely with research and development (R&D), manufacturing or engineering, project management, finance, sales, marketing, legal, operations, and customer service. They will be looking to you to develop and maintain a prioritized list of market requirements that continually improve your products' performance and the financial return to your organization. You'll be expected to create and manage a rolling tactical roadmap that outlines what customers can expect from you and your team going forward. As the person responsible for your products, you'll make the final decisions regarding the ultimate approval of product design, functional requirements, and changes from envisioned scope. Because you control final approval of the design and scope, and likely recommend the pricing strategy, you must also be sure products release according to the roadmap schedule and that your products reach their financial targets.

All the way through this process, you'll be responsible for leading cross-functional collaboration efforts across the organization in support of your product objectives. You'll also interact externally with customers, prospects, analysts, and business partners. These interactions may include focus groups, advisory committees, surveys, or customer visits.

As your products move through the development process, upper management will expect you to provide training and support to internal stake holders who interact with the customers that use your products. Colleagues will draw on your market knowledge to support product launches and go-to-market activities and to help develop content to support the sales process and sales collateral. The sales organization will count on you to help close business with key customers.

Finally, the executive team will expect you to establish and communicate performance metrics for your products and report progress versus plan.

TRANSITION SHOCK: CHANGING FUNCTIONS REQUIRES A CHANGE IN THE WAY YOU THINK

Individuals like Sean, who come into product management from functions like sales or customer service, often experience a sense of transition shock at the change in perspective. Because product management is a function that by necessity takes a wider bird's eye view of market needs, product managers tend to think longer term as well.

This contrasts sharply with the functional perspective of the sales team, which is asked to think quarter to quarter, client to client, or deal to deal as they focus on their sales plan. This also holds true for entrants to product management from customer service, where resolving client needs quickly and satisfactorily is the name of the game. As a result, the shift from these functions into a product management role can be a bit of a shock. You'll need to adjust how you think about timeframes, and you may initially miss the sense of immediacy that came from your previous role.

If, like Sean, you're now feeling a cold sweat mixed with excitement as you come to understand the full range of responsibilities that you've accepted, it is understandable. Product management is a big job and one that is vital to your organization's success as it grows and prospers. Remember, knowledge is power and the more you know of what your colleagues expect of you, the more you'll be able to take the reins, step into this leadership role, and successfully manage their expectations.

CHALLENGES YOU CAN EXPECT TO ENCOUNTER

As you begin your role as a product manager, you can expect to face a variety of challenges while you accumulate the necessary information to craft a vision and execute your tactical plans. Some of the challenges will be created internally. Others will result from the changing nature of dynamic markets and competitors. Either way, you'll learn to be nimble and make necessary adjustments as circumstances require. Let's take a closer look at some of the challenges you're likely to face.

TIME CONSTRAINTS

As you transition into your new role, you'll draw heavily on your existing knowledge about the market and customer needs. However, your base knowledge stepping into the role will go only so far. You'll likely find that you need to supplement that knowledge quickly as people inside and outside your organization increasingly look to you as the definitive expert on your product and your market. Accumulating and processing the necessary information takes time. It's not likely that you will have all the time needed as you step into the role. Your role was created to help address existing or foreseeable challenges your company is facing or to capitalize on tangible market opportunities. As a result, you'll be pulled in several directions simultaneously as you work to address immediate needs, construct a vision, and put the pieces in place for the longer term.

FALLING INTO THE TRAP OF BEING REACTIVE RATHER THAN PROACTIVE

With all the demands on your time, it's easy to get caught in the trap of allocating too much time toward addressing "hot button" issues versus steering your products toward your objective. Customer service, sales, finance, engineering, and others will all be bidding for your time. It's all too easy to cede control to the immediate needs. If you prioritize the immediate over the key factors that will ensure that you attain your organization's business objectives, it's unlikely that you'll be successful. Learning to allocate most of your time to the 20 percent of activities that drive the highest probability of your organization's success (the "80/20" rule) will be essential to *your* success. Your goal is to avoid the trap of the immediate while remaining responsive to the needs of others. You can do this by putting in place a proactive plan in which you can manage immediate needs while focusing on what is truly essential for your organizations success first. More on this later...

LACK OF CONTROL

Many product managers do not have profit and loss responsibility and must rely on influence and consensus building skills to be successful. This is particularly true in start-ups and mid-sized organizations. The lack of profit and loss responsibility often creates challenges, because your effectiveness is dependent, to some degree, on others' good will and shared market objectives. Control is not essential for success as a product manager. But to be successful managing through influence, you must thoughtfully involve others in your product management activities and give them a voice in the processes you construct as you drive your product to market success.

TENSION BETWEEN SHORT-TERM REVENUE AND LONGER-TERM OBJECTIVES

As a product manager you'll be executing on a three- to five-year product strategy and a shorter term tactical execution plan that covers a rolling 12 months. Others in your organization will be working on more immediate objectives. Tension will arise when their immediate needs occasionally rub up against your longer term plan. Transparency, objective facts, and level-headedness will help you manage through these challenges. It will also help you to look at the issue from the other person's perspective while working to resolve conflicts. Occasionally, executive management may need to make a decision regarding which timeframe's objective is more important.

DIFFERENCES OF OPINION REGARDING THE DIRECTION OF YOUR PRODUCTS

Politics is an inevitable consequence of forming organizations. And it is inevitable that someone within your organization will have a strong opinion — different from your own — about the direction your products should take. Many times this happens when someone else had control of your product's direction before you assumed your new role. Or, it could be that this individual interacts with customers and has simply come to a different conclusion.

Either way, managing through situations like this requires facts. Often when someone challenges the direction you're taking they are acting more on intuition than facts. But *facts rule* when it comes to managing through the inevitable disagreements.

While it can be difficult, it is important that you don't take these challenges personally — even if the other party does. Remember, even though the other person doesn't agree with the direction you're taking your product, they likely believe that what they are advocating is in the organization's best interest, just as you do. If possible, try to understand the other person's perspective. Dissonant views often provide insight into something that you need to better understand and that just might improve your existing plan.

CHANGING MARKET DYNAMICS

Markets live and breathe. They are uncaring when it comes to the plan you've put in place to grow your product. New competitors rise to the fore, old ones reinvent themselves, and customers' needs change with time. The work you do as a product manager to understand your market and the trends as well as to identify potential risks should help insulate your business from nasty shocks. However, the unexpected can happen. When it does, you'll need to correct your course quickly.

WHAT TYPE OF MARKET ARE YOU TRYING TO SERVE?

As a product manager, it is very important to answer the question, what type of market am I working in?

Existing markets — the playing field has identifiable competitors with entrenched market positions. The customer is well known.

Resegmented markets — you are attempting to carve out a piece of an existing market by offering a lower-priced product than your competitors or by targeting a segment of an existing market that plays to your product's unique strengths.

New markets — you are attempting to create a large base of entirely new customers by serving an emerging or unmet need. New markets have little or no competition.

SKILLS TO SUCCEED

Just as the role of a product manager covers a wide range of responsibilities, you'll need to draw upon a wide range of skills to be successful. The abilities that you'll need to have or develop fall into two separate categories: functional competencies, or *hard skills*, and behavioral competencies, commonly called *soft skills*. Let's take a moment and examine the difference between these competencies before we discuss the skills themselves.

Hard skills are the technical skills needed to be successful in a position. These skills relate directly to your education and experience. Many of these skills, for example, your ability to work with spreadsheet software or manage your time, can be taught. However, hard skills alone will not enable you to be successful. You will need to work closely with others to achieve your organization's business objectives, and for that, you'll need soft skills.

Soft skills, or behavioral competencies, are the skills that help you develop relationships with others and contribute to your organization's success. They tend to be attributes such as your social behavior, your communication ability, personal habits, your degree of friendliness, and your attitude.

Think of hard and soft skills as complementary skills that are *both* required to successfully do your job. Sean, at Alpha Technology Ventures, was selected as the new product manager by his CEO Sinclair because of at least three qualities he displayed. One was a hard skill, learned through experience — the ability to understand in-depth the company's new product. The other two were the soft skills of intuitively understanding each customer's needs and the emotional maturity to never over commit. While these are by no means the only skills that make Sean or any product manager successful in their role, they do demonstrate the importance of having both sets of skills to be successful. Now let's take a closer look at these skills as they relate to successful product managers.

PRODUCT PROFIT AND LOSS STATEMENT (P&L)

What is a product profit and loss statement and why does it matter? A product P&L is a financial statement used by product managers to determine whether a product or family of products and services are making or losing money over a specified period; for example, weekly, monthly, quarterly, annually, year-to-date, or year over year. The profit and loss statement illustrates how revenue — money received from the sale of the company's products and services — becomes net income. Net income is what is left after all expenses have been deducted from the revenue the company has received. Profit and loss statements help product managers identify problem areas — including expenses, sales, and margins — that can be investigated or corrected in a timely fashion.

THE FUNCTIONAL COMPETENCIES OF A PRODUCT MANAGER

The functional skills listed below range from the most basic — like computer skills — to more evolved skills, such as profit and loss management. Stepping into your new role you will likely find, like Sean, that possessing several of these functional skills will be enough to begin your way down the path to future success. However, you'll quickly need to understand product development, new product capability or market identification, and budgeting. Profit and loss (P&L) capabilities depend highly on your company's stage of growth. It may be some time before you need to demonstrate skill in managing a P&L.

- **Computer skills** — The most common computer applications used by product managers are spreadsheet, presentation, and flow charting software. However, as your organization becomes increasingly more successful you'll find that more specialized software is important. An example is mind mapping software, which can be used to capture data from brainstorming sessions.

- **Time management** — Given all the activities competing for your attention, you'll need to be constantly aware of how you use your time.

- **Process establishment** — You will likely discover, as you step into your role, that there is a shortage of process underlying your organization's product management efforts. Putting logical frameworks in place lets you achieve the results your executive team expects. These frameworks will be essential to your success and will help you effectively manage your time.

- **Product development process knowledge** — Product managers need to work closely with engineers and manufacturing teams as partners. To gain their respect, you'll have to quickly come up to speed on their current processes, develop relationships with your counterparts, and participate actively in the product development process.

- **Ability to identify new product capabilities or markets** — As you step into your new position, you'll need to invest time in better understanding your market — the trends and the competitors — and take an inventory of your own organization's capabilities. As you consolidate this information and visit with clients, you'll discover opportunities to improve your product's market position and identify new product and market opportunities.

- **Budgeting** — As the product management function grows, budgeting will become more important. Budgeting money to operate and achieve your business objectives will become part of your routine.

- **Profit and loss** — To manage a profit and loss statement, you'll need a deep understanding of how the elements of your business are interconnected and the underlying implications of making changes to your products.

THE BEHAVIORAL COMPETENCIES OF A PRODUCT MANAGER

Hard skills are often viewed as the fundamental building blocks required to do a job. Behavioral, or soft skills, shape how effective you'll be in your position. Let's look more closely at the wide range of soft skills that you'll need as a product manager.

- **Strategic** — The skill to find the best path to reaching your goal. Strategic skills are especially valuable when coupled with the tactical skills you'll need to execute your strategy.

- **Conceptual** — Your ability to take complex or disparate pieces of information and rearrange them in new ways that simplify and convey essential information in terms that are easier to understand.

- **Entrepreneurial** — The ability to identify and take new ideas to market and create value. This skill requires a certain degree of prudent risk-taking as you pursue value creation in the hopes of creating new product innovations or breakthrough products.

- **Creative thinking** — This skill requires looking at problems in unconventional ways that allow you to discover new opportunities to disrupt the status quo.

- **Anticipating problems** — This skill requires you to think several steps ahead and calculate possible outcomes with a focus on smoothing the path to achievement of your plan or your team's objectives. Whether anticipating obstacles in your path as you execute your plan or removing obstacles before your team encounters them, this skill is essential for your success.

- **Analytic** — Product managers deal with difficult problems that are not easily solved. You will need analytic skills to breakdown and solve complex problems without the benefit of all the necessary information. Analytic skills are commonly used to evaluate market opportunities, assess competitive threats, put a plan of action into place, and manage financial information.

- **Political astuteness** — Because product managers work cross-functionally and touch every area of a business, being sensitive to your political environment is a necessity that will make you more effective. Your ability to understand the internal political dynamic and manage through it will help you get the results your organization requires.

- **Customer skills** — Because your central mission is to understand customer needs and act as their representative inside your organization, you'll spend much time interacting with customers. Good listening skills, transparency, and following through on commitments create trust. These are the building blocks of developing strong and flourishing customer relationships.

- **Results orientation** — Your ability to get results is one of the most important gauges of how successful you are as a product manager. However, it is important to remember that how you achieve your results is often as important as the result itself.

- **Interpersonal skills** — Your ability to interact with people in ways that build trust and help your organization achieve its objectives. Because most product managers rely heavily on influence skills to achieve results, your ability to work with others to achieve mutually beneficial results will be important to your individual success.

- **Leadership** — Others will look to you for leadership and direction. Although there is no single definition of leadership, it is generally accepted that leadership encompasses the ability to align others toward a shared goal by inspiring trust and confidence. Your ability to listen to others, respect their opinions — even if they differ with your own — and incorporate them in your processes, and back up your decisions with facts will go a long way in building the trusting relationships essential to your long-term success.

- **Cross-functional collaboration** — The ability to work with representatives from the various functional areas of your company, at all levels. Many times this will simply require a straightforward one-on-one meeting with someone from another functional area to solve less complex challenges. For more complex challenges, you'll need representation from all the functional areas.

Your ability to both lead and contribute to the various cross-functional initiatives within your organization will pay dividends.

- **Influence skills** — The ability to achieve results without relying on direct control or position power to achieve a desired outcome. You will utilize this skill in all facets of your position as a product manager.

- **Calm under pressure** — Circumstances will occasionally conspire to pull you off center. It can be difficult to hold your composure in the face of intense pressure, but this skill is important to maintain your credibility. It's not uncommon for product managers to come under pressure over their decisions about markets, customers, or requirements. Others will lose their composure and react emotionally to your decisions. It is guaranteed to happen more than once in your career. Take a deep breath and do not let them pull you off your center. Remember, how you deal with adversity demonstrates your character. Few people want to follow someone who loses their cool.

DISRUPTIVE

This term is commonly used to describe an innovative idea or product that upsets the status quo and therefore is particularly threatening to companies that hold significant market share or a market leadership position.

Disruptive originated with Clayton Christensen, a professor of business administration at the Harvard Business School, well known for his study of innovation in commercial enterprises.

BALANCING COMPETING PRIORITIES

Because your role entails interacting with functional counterparts from across the organization, you will rapidly find yourself at the center of a variety of competing priorities. Some will further your product line objectives, and others will not. The requests for your time and attention will range from answering a question raised by a customer service representative as a result of an inbound client call, to addressing a concern raised by a member of the board regarding how you calculated your market share position.

These interactions result from your position as the central repository of knowledge and expertise on your market and product. Figure 2–1 provides a visual of the interplay between these relationships. As a product manager, you are the central source for information, the hub. You will interact with every functional area, and as the illustration notes, the interaction is two-way.

FIGURE 2-1. FUNCTIONAL VIEW OF THE HUB AND SPOKE NATURE OF PRODUCT MANAGEMENT

Let's walk through some quick examples of these two-way interactions. As a product manager, you'll seek information from the sales organization regarding customer needs and competitors. In turn, the sales organization will want you to give them information about the direction of the market and your product.

Customer service will send you information on defects or bugs and service requests and alert you to hot button issues that require immediate triage. In return, they will expect you to be responsive to their needs and educate them about market trends, competitors, and product information.

In the case of the finance department, you will likely ask them to help you model different pricing scenarios or with reports that evaluate how your products are performing against expectations. Finance will look to you for pricing recommendations that impact their financial models and forecasts on what you anticipate sales to look like.

As you can see from just these three examples, each functional area of the business is a valuable partner and a source of important tools and information that help you achieve your product objectives. However, you can also clearly see how your time will become compressed as others, in support of the common objective of growing your product's revenues, ask for large segments of your time.

To successfully balance these competing priorities and requests, you must ask two key questions:

- Does this request help us attain the company's product objectives more quickly?
- Will supporting this request enable you to become more efficient by reducing future or redundant requests for your time?

If the answer to these questions is yes, then the request needs to be moved to the top of your list. Remember, the 80/20 rule applies. You want to make sure that your time is applied *first* to those things that will help you attain your objectives and/or make you more efficient by reducing future demands on your time. Keep in mind, however, that just because something doesn't make the top of your list doesn't mean it should be ignored. Others are relying on you to help achieve their objectives. Withholding support can come back to haunt you when you need their support the most!

The hub and spoke diagram helps to conceptualize the two-way nature of product management. An influence map is another tool you can use to help successfully manage your time. As we discussed in chapter one, all organizations are not the same. Start-ups have different organizational needs than mature companies. Influence maps are most helpful in understanding key contributors in larger and more complex organizations and less so in a start-up environment.

What is an influence map? It is an easy way to visualize those people who will be the most important contributors to your product's success. It's easy to take for granted that you know who these people are within your organization. However, after doing this exercise you may come to a different conclusion.

The map you're about to draw is a simplified version of a standard influence map, which will suffice for our purposes. Take a blank sheet of paper and a pencil — make sure it is a pencil — because you'll likely move names around once you start to map things out. Now draw three concentric circles: the smallest at the center and the other two increasingly larger circles surrounding the center circle.

This is illustrated in Figure 2–2. The circle in the center is you and your product. Label the second largest circle "critical to success" — this person will be critical for your product's success. Label the largest circle "important to success."

FIGURE 2–2. INFLUENCE MAP

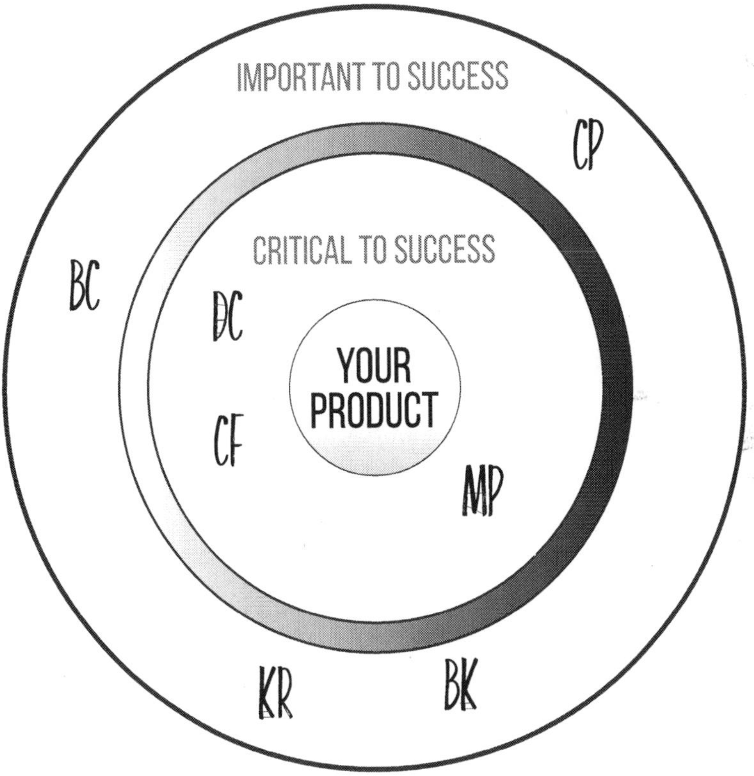

Now pause for a second and take a mental inventory of the people that you believe are most important to your product's future success. They could be your boss, the CEO, a sales support specialist, or anyone else. Place the initials of those who are most important to your product's success closest in the critical circle. Others, whose support is important, should be placed in the third concentric circle.

Once you have drawn the map and are satisfied with the result, put it down and think of one or two other people that you trust and who know the organization well. Take the diagram to them and ask for their input individually. They will likely point out something you failed to consider and may even suggest erasing a name or moving a set of initials from the critical circle to the important or vice versa. When you have the final map in hand, burn in your mind the images of the people you're relying on for your product's success. Add this as an additional prioritization filter to incoming requests.

Combine your influence map and the key questions we discussed earlier, and you'll be well armed to thoughtfully balance the competing requests for your time and the challenges and exciting opportunities that lie ahead.

STOP! DON'T THROW AWAY THAT INFLUENCE MAP, IT HAS OTHER USES!

Hold on to your influence map. As we will see in later chapters, you'll want to reference your map as you begin to form your own cross-functional teams in pursuit of your objectives. The influence map is a handy tool to ensure that you include the right people down the road.

CONSENSUS BUILDING AND CROSS-FUNCTIONAL TEAMS

We have spent significant time in this chapter discussing product management's cross-functional nature. Your ability to understand each functional area's frame of reference and what they are tasked with achieving is important as you ask for their time. Many problems that you'll encounter cannot be solved by working within the functional boundaries of a single department. Complex challenges will require representatives from the various functions, at all levels, to come together as a team. Your ability to work productively with others toward a common objective and get the best out of your collaboration is essential to your success.

Cross-functional teams sometimes rely on consensus building to resolve an issue. Consensus is a form of decision making that results when team members collectively agree on a path to resolve a shared problem. Consensus decisions have an embedded power because usually no single person is driving the decision, although they may be influencing the outcome. Because the participants in consensus building have voluntarily agreed to the decision, they are very likely to support its implementation after the meeting is over.

If the meeting's goal is to reach consensus, a facilitator should avoid using position power — reliance on job title or position within the organizational structure — as a means to achieve an outcome. Relying on position power has its down sides. Others may resist a ram-rodded decision either in the meeting or during implementation. As a product manager, because your constant involvement with various aspects of the business creates established relationships with the functional areas and their representatives, you may be called upon to be a facilitator. The key to good facilitation is to not allow your biases to impact the decisions too heavily, and to make sure everyone's voice is heard.

CHAPTER TWO'S TIPS FOR TAKING CHARGE

- Product managers are responsible for the overall success of their product. In start-ups and some mid-sized companies, product managers often rely on influence skills to achieve their objectives. In larger organizations, product managers may control the profit and loss statement which provides more direct control over decision making.

- The central mission of product managers is to know their markets, customers' needs, competitors, and trends better than anyone else in the organization. Your objective is to collect information from a variety of sources and focus on what is most important based upon the best data and facts available. It is important for you to not be too heavily swayed by any one point of view as you make decisions about your product.

- Given the breadth of the job, you'll find that you have to draw upon a variety of skills to address the challenges and capitalize on the exciting opportunities that lie ahead. It is equally important that you understand what is expected of you in your new role and who you'll need to work with closely to achieve your objectives.

- Effectively managing your time in a position that has so many cross-functional connections can be quite challenging. To ensure that you're prioritizing your time effectively, ask yourself two key questions: will this incoming request for your time further your organizations product objectives and will it enable you to become more efficient by reducing future or redundant requests for your time? If the answer is yes, move it to the top of your priorities.

CHAPTER THREE: KEY ACTIVITIES TO HELP YOU SUCCEED

The car door closed tightly with a reassuring thud.

Sinclair's mind began to play back Alpha Technology Ventures' seventh off-site board meeting, which had just wrapped up. "Almost everything had gone as planned," he concluded. Sinclair was thankful for his strong and supportive board. All nine board members were significant contributors to the company's success and although the conversations were often lively, they never crossed the line and became personally confrontational. There was good chemistry on the board and a broad base of industry experience. Sinclair glanced upward and thanked his lucky stars. His mood soured momentarily as he thought back to the first company he had run, which had not enjoyed that luxury. "Well, nobody had said my job was going to be easy," he reflected, only half jokingly.

During the board meeting there had been one "flare up," as Sinclair liked to call it, when the board members pressed him particularly hard on a topic. Worse, it had been completely unexpected. "It just goes to show that no matter how well you plan you can never fully anticipate all of the possible scenarios," he thought to himself. As Sinclair started the car and pulled out into the light traffic, he continued to mull over the resulting discussion.

Although the meeting had been a success, the flare up still troubled him and he was not completely sure why. Behind the steering wheel he let his mind wander over his feelings and some of the reasons started to surface. He had gone to great lengths to personally call every board member to go over each of the topics and to flesh out any items that might need additional advance preparation. None of the board members had raised the flare up as an issue. Sinclair was even more troubled by the fact that he had committed a rare stumble when he tried, unsuccessfully, to address the topic. That bothered him the most!

The flare up had occurred during an off-topic conversation regarding the new product management function that he had launched earlier this week. Every board member was completely behind the initiative; that had not even been an issue during the meeting. The problem occurred when Sinclair had been asked by one of the board members to describe what the board could expect from the new product management function. Notoriously hard on himself, Sinclair knew he had given a less-than-clear response to the question. Unfortunately for everyone the conversation had snowballed. "Why," he asked himself, "had I not seen this coming?" In hindsight he knew he should have anticipated the question. Thankfully, two of the most respected board members who had been in the technology business for years, as well as Kevin Knowles, the chairman of the board, had stepped in and attempted to answer the question.

Kevin had pointed out that Sinclair was doing a great job and reminded the entire board that they had been pushing Sinclair to step back from day-to-day involvement with the product so he could invest more time in scaling the business. Kevin went on to say that in several of the other businesses he had been involved in *the addition of a product management function had served as the primary catalyst for creating sustainable growth.*

As Sinclair pulled into his driveway, the thing that kept troubling him rose to the surface. It was the way the discussion ended. The chairman had resolved the snowballing conversation by suggesting that the new product manager participate in the annual management team review with the board at the end of the year. With everyone in agreement, Kevin knowingly reassured the rest of the board that when it came to product management *"you will know it when you see it."*

The resolution was a good one, but Sinclair was still unsettled. *Why had it been so hard to explain what to expect?* As Sinclair turned off his car, he made a mental note to give Sean a "heads up" first thing tomorrow morning about his future participation in the annual management team review with the board.

The following morning, Sinclair stopped by Sean's desk and shared the news about his upcoming involvement in the annual management team review with the board.

Although Sean had attempted to put on a brave face, it was clear he was concerned about how fast expectations were growing regarding his new role. Sean appeared somewhat reassured by Sinclair's insistence that he would do whatever was necessary between now and the year-end review to support Sean's success.

To demonstrate his willingness to help Sean, Sinclair had decided to share the company's business plan after making sure that Sean would keep it confidential. Both he and Sean knew there was a lot of work to do between now and the end of the year. Sinclair had tremendous faith in Sean, but Sean was going to have to quickly roll up his sleeves and dig in. As Sinclair turned the corner and walked out of sight, he heard Sean unconsciously ask himself, "Where do I start?"

IMMERSE YOURSELF IN YOUR ORGANIZATION'S OBJECTIVES

The best way to understand the assumptions that underlie your new position as a product manager is to read your organization's business plan. A business plan is a document, often created to attract investment capital, that outlines your company's business objectives and the logic behind them. It includes a detailed set of activities illustrating how your company intends to achieve its goals. The author of this plan was likely your CEO or the most senior member of your company. The business plan has also likely been shared with the senior leadership of your organization, potential investors, and the board of directors.

TAKE YOUR ORGANIZATION'S CULTURAL TEMPERATURE BEFORE YOU REQUEST THE BUSINESS PLAN

Before you ask for a copy of your company's business plan, you'll need to take the temperature of your organization's culture. Given its sensitivity, not all companies will be willing to share this information. If you don't believe your company will, there are a couple of other avenues you can pursue.

Your first alternative is to ask for only those elements of the business plan that relate directly to your products. Given that you've been tasked with leading your company's product management efforts and this information has a direct bearing on your day-to-day position, your colleagues may be more open to this approach.

If that option is not feasible, don't worry. In Chapter Four, we'll discuss another approach that will allow you, on your own, to begin assembling much of the same information in your company's business plan.

The format of your company's business plan varies based upon the document's goal and the business's complexity. The more complex the business, the greater the length of the plan. Most business plans range from 15 to 50 pages. Although the length may vary, well written business plans strive to be concise and to the point. The most common elements of a business plan include:

- Executive summary
- About the company and industry
- Market dynamics
- Technology/manufacturing/ operations

- Administration, organization, and people
- Key milestones
- Risks to the business
- Financial data

Now, let's look more closely at the information contained in each of the sections to better understand how it can help you quickly scale the learning curve. All business plans begin with an executive summary. This section gives a consolidated view of the most important information in the document. It often begins with a brief description of the business, the products, and the markets served.

It also outlines what will be sold, to whom, and why customers will buy from your organization instead of your competition. Important financial data, such as projected revenue, profits, cash flows, and return on investment (ROI), will be showcased. The summary will also outline what type of financial resources the company anticipates using and explains how the money will be spent. It will also detail the company's current business position and any essential developments within the company that are important to the overall success of the plan.

The second section of the business plan will overview your company and the industry your company focuses on — beginning with the current state and looking into the future. Important information about industry trends that will positively or negatively impact your company's business will be discussed. It is also customary to briefly describe the history of your company and how it fits into the context of the larger industry. This section will also outline the products and services your company intends to market with a focus on the unique aspects of your offering that make it compelling and that will keep customers from going to competitors.

The market dynamics segment explains how your company sees its market or markets in terms of size, structure, growth rates, and potential market share. This

RETURN ON INVESTMENT

Return on investment, or ROI, is a term you'll come to know well as a product manager. It is one of the most common metrics used to evaluate, understand, and compare investment options. Once calculated, it expresses the profit or loss resulting from an investment as an annual percentage of return. The formula for calculating ROI is:

$$ROI = \frac{(Gain\, from\, Investment - Cost\, of\, Investment)}{Cost\, of\, Investment}$$

Products that have a high ROI are desirable but may spur competitors to enter your market. Products with low or negative ROI are generally phased out or bypassed as an investment option if better options with higher ROI are available.

section overviews your company's market strategy and the positioning it will use to capitalize on perceived market opportunities. It will also contain estimates on the size of your primary competitor's market share and describe how they approach the market. Product pricing will be outlined along with the logic that led to the pricing strategy being developed. This section will mention who your company sells to and the distribution channels that will be used to get your products to paying customers. It will lay out what marketing tools will speed up adoption of your products or services (example: public relations, promotions, etc.). It will also outline projected sales revenue, usually over three to five years.

The technology/manufacturing/operations segment describes the design of your company's products and the budget implemented to enable the company to hit its financial goals. It will also detail the process being used to produce your products and describe the resident expertise that enables the production process to happen. Procedures will be outlined including how resources are allocated, the product production process steps, and the key dates for anticipated product deliverables. This section also includes a product development budget that comprises all the expenses required to design the product and put it into production.

The administration, organization, and people part of the plan addresses how the business will be run and organized as well as how your company plans to retain talented team members so it can attain its business plan. This section includes how the company sets up administration functions such as policies and controls, the organizational structure, and the management philosophy. It will also detail how the company intends to scale the number of people required over a period of time — typically three years.

The key milestones portion conveys specific deliverable dates that have already occurred, as well as those that still need to occur as the company executes its plan. These could include raising capital, locating office space, hiring key staff, developing a prototype, and signing agreements with preferred distribution partners. The seminal milestones are often visually represented in a chart to make understanding the sequence of events that need to occur easy to understand.

TREAT THE INFORMATION YOU'VE BEEN GIVEN WITH RESPECT

The information contained in a business plan is highly confidential and must be treated that way. If your senior leadership has allowed you to see the plan, they are placing a great deal of trust in you. Only discuss the details of the business plan with those people who also have been granted access by your company's senior leadership. It is best to establish these ground rules at the time you receive permission to read the plan.

The risks section details those elements of the plan that are subject to being derailed. Risks can include regulatory factors, market changes, new competitors, legal challenges, funding issues, or a variety of other elements. This section of the plan not only lays out the potential risks to the plan but what the company intends to do to negate the risks.

The final section of the business plan outlines the financial data and assumptions that support attaining the business objectives. This section generally consists of a cash flow statement, an income statement (company profit and loss statement), and a balance sheet. All three of these financial statements share common data and are linked. However, while the data are linked, each financial statement illustrates a different perspective relating to the health of the business.

The income statement shows the estimated cash-generating ability of the business and the resulting gains or losses in revenue and profit. The cash flow statement demonstrates how much cash is required to cover expenses and the timing of when it will be used, as well as where the money will come from. The third financial statement is the balance sheet, which illustrates an annual view of the business covering assets, liabilities, and equity.

Now that we have reviewed the various sections of a business plan, I'm sure it's increasingly clear why this is an excellent place for you to start. First and foremost, there is no better place to accumulate a 360-degree view of your company's business.

The business plan overviews the critical logic and assumptions that underlie the success of the business and your product. It presents the business in a holistic way, but outlines important information from different vantages: financial, marketing, sales, etc. It also details the industry trends, company risks, and milestones that you'll likely need to know to be successful.

Most importantly, there is simply no better way to see the company and market *through your CEO's eyes*. To be successful you'll need to acquire knowledge quickly and thoroughly. The information in the business plan describes how your senior leadership views the company, your market, and your product. You could spend endless hours talking to your CEO or the functional leaders of your business in an effort to piece together the original assumptions about the business. But why do that when there is one document that can quickly bring you up to speed and give you the same results?

If we take a look at the information that is available in the business plan and compare it to the knowledge that Sean brought from his previous position in sales, we quickly see that he knew bits and pieces of information contained in the business plan. Sean likely knew the names of the competitors, what they typically charged for their offerings, and how they positioned their product. However, Sean likely had just as many blind spots as bits of knowledge. His prior job didn't require him to know about the company's product development process, the costs of developing his product, the pricing rationale, and so forth. Having access to the business plan enables you to quickly fill in information that would take significantly longer to assemble on your own, enabling you to add value to your organization more quickly.

UNDERSTANDING YOUR COMPANY'S GROWTH STAGE AND ITS IMPACT

The role of a product manager is not one size fits all. Each stage of company growth places emphasis on those skills that are best suited to achieve a desired outcome. Perhaps one of the best ways to understand the degrees of emphasis placed on the skills that make up your role at each stage of company growth, is to *look at your role from the perspective of what your company is trying to accomplish with its product activities*. The objectives generally fall into two categories: *creating new value* through innovation or *augmenting existing value*. Let's begin this examination by looking more closely at a start-up company.

GROWTH STAGE: START-UP

The primary mission of a start-up company is to correctly identify a market opportunity and successfully iterate with customers until a scalable product is developed and brought to market. This process relies heavily on active customer engagement and rapid cycle trial and error. The objective is to attract a core base of early adopters for your product that can be turned into a larger mass market client base over time.

To achieve this objective, *start-ups focus on creating new value through innovation*. A high degree of flexibility is required to succeed as your assumptions about the market and customer needs are continually challenged.

Because innovation is the central mantra of the organization at this stage of growth, emphasis is placed on those skills that enable innovation to occur. These skills include but are not limited to:

- Creative thinking
- Entrepreneurial spirit
- Conceptual and analytic abilities
- Customer focus
- Teamwork

Administrative skills such as budgeting and profit and loss management have less value in a start-up, as the company is still in its infancy and is not yet mature enough to require those skills outside of the core leadership. As a product manager you'll be spending a large percentage of your time face to face with potential clients and new customers as the company constantly iterates its initial prototype in an effort to attract more customers. Because the product iteration cycles will likely happen very quickly, significant amounts of your time will also be spent working closely with the development team. Detailed processes are intentionally kept to a bare minimum so as not to slow down progress. Time is of the essence as your company attempts to utilize its limited resources in the most efficient means possible. Because the organizational structure of most start-ups is flat, you'll take hands-on responsibility for the full spectrum of product management-related activities from market needs identification to developing the launch plan for the initial product. Job specialization is very limited given the resource-constrained nature of this stage of growth.

EARLY ADOPTERS AND THE MASS MARKET

As products evolve, so does your customer base. Companies actively seek early adopters for new products. Early adopters are highly valued for two reasons: they are a vital source of constructive input during a product's development, and they provide an early source of revenue. An early adopter is generally defined as a person or company that is among the first to purchase a new product or service. Early adopters are willing to assume a degree of risk in order to be one of the first to use your product or service. In return, they expect to have a voice in how the product continues to develop by directly providing input as the company continues to refine its offering.

As products become more mature they are better positioned to expand beyond the initial early adopter client base. This evolution prompts product managers and marketers to target the much larger mass market. The term mass market is used to describe the larger segment of mainstream customers and the increased revenue they represent. Unlike early adopters, mass market clients require a "complete" product. They tend to be more pragmatic and are less interested in taking risks in return for a larger voice in the development process.

GROWTH STAGE: MID-SIZED

Contrast this with the primary mission of a successful mid-sized company. While a start-up's mantra is centered on innovation and identifying early adopters, *thriving mid-sized companies focus a significant amount of resources on augmenting their existing products to ensure continued high rates of growth.* Your company is now tapping into the mass market and attempting to bring along the early adopters that initially made it successful. However, your new mass market customers are looking for "complete" products with all the bells and whistles, unlike the early adopters, who were happy to have the minimum set of required capabilities and a large voice in how the product evolved. Managing high growth and sustaining your existing products requires a different configuration of your skills. Emphasis is placed on different skills:

- Strategic
- Process development
- Cross-functional engagement
- Anticipating problems
- Calm under pressure

- Leadership

- Budgeting

As the company grew out of the start-up phase, it added staff and complexity. Establishing a budget and effectively managing it has become a standard part of your role. You're now spending a significant amount of time with customers, but the variety of activities has increased significantly. In the start-up phase, most of your time was spent iterating with customers. Now you also host an advisory committee, contribute to client conferences, participate in selling to key clients, and support regional customer meetings. Customer engagement is more structured. You still devote a large percentage of your time to the development team and development activities, but the amount of people involved and the complexity has increased.

Customers are expecting to see a product roadmap and are holding you accountable for consistent execution against established expectations. The development process, while nimble, is also more structured as you now must manage the expectations of a large customer base. As the company grew, so did the need for processes that support effective coordination across the organization. The organizational structure is no longer as flat as it once was. You're still responsible for the full span of product management duties, but now there is more specialized support and you're overseeing rather than doing certain aspects of the job. Things have changed.

DON'T TAKE THE NEED TO ACKNOWLEDGE AND RESPOND TO CUSTOMER FEEDBACK LIGHTLY!

Regardless of whether you choose to invest in a customer's suggestion, it's important to have a system in place to acknowledge their suggestion and to explain what you intend to do with it. Many organizations ask for client input, but you would be shocked to find out how few of them acknowledge the feedback and update their customers on what they plan to do with it! Not acknowledging incoming suggestions on how your products can be improved can make your customers think you aren't listening or don't care — neither of which is good for your business.

GROWTH STAGE: MATURE

In the final phase of company growth, a mature company, *augmenting and innovation skills are both required.* Mature companies seek steady and predictable growth, which becomes increasingly difficult as your company grows. Having captured significant market share for its products, augmenting the existing products and revenue streams is very important. However, to continue to achieve the ever-increasing growth and revenue targets, larger organizations need to look for innovation opportunities — organically, via partnerships, or through merger and acquisitions. This requires a broad array of skills:

- Strategic
- Leadership
- Political astuteness
- Analytic
- Highly developed interpersonal skills
- Cross-functional abilities
- Profit and loss
- Calm under pressure

MATRIXED WORK ENVIRONMENTS

Matrixed is used by organizations to describe a work setting where individuals function under a dual authority system. In other words, this is a style of management where one individual has two reporting superiors: a functional boss, for example a vice president of engineering, and an operational boss, a product manager. The functional boss manages the payroll and performance aspects of the relationship, while the operational boss may be directing the employees' day-to-day activities as part of a team or project.

As a product manager, you will often work in matrixed environments where members of your product team have a direct reporting relationship outside of your function. A matrixed relationship is also commonly called a "dotted line" because this is usually how the operational relationship is portrayed on organizational charts.

Organizational complexity has continued to increase at this stage of growth. Your company is now likely operating overseas and the consequences of the decisions you make has increased significantly. Client engagement is a large component of your job and it continues to be very structured as your time is at a premium. Development activities span multiple locations and time zones and still remain central to your day-to-day activities.

Well documented and adhered to processes have been deployed. The organizational structure is more complex as you interact with a wide variety of parties across the enterprise in pursuit of your objectives. You're responsible for the entire product management process but you work through a team of direct reports and matrixed individuals, including contractors. The degree of specialization is high and you are able to draw on experts in specific areas to aid your execution.

As you can see, each stage of growth has its own primary focus and requires a different use of your skills. Recognizing the difference between innovation activities and augmenting activities is very important and can help you decide which product management approach you want to use.

DIFFERENT PRODUCT MANAGEMENT APPROACHES

There is more than one product management approach available for you to choose from. The options include:

- Capturing the voice of the customer
- Workflow analysis
- Outcome-driven innovation

The voice of the customer, or customer-driven, approach relies heavily on *what customers tell you they want*. The work flow approach relies on what you observe about *how customers do their job*. The outcomes approach focuses on *what customers are striving to achieve and the metrics they use to define success*. To select the right approach, or quite possibly the right combination of options, it helps to think back to what you learned about your company's objectives from the business plan and overlay your knowledge about whether your company is primarily focused on augmenting, innovating, or both. Let's walk through the three approaches in more detail.

CAPTURING THE VOICE OF THE CUSTOMER

The voice of the customer approach is based on the principle that if you listen to your customers they will tell you what you need to do to create new products and improve your existing products. This method of capturing product requirements grew out of the much broader process improvement movement that took root in the 1980s and 90s.

As the process improvement movement took hold, companies began actively seeking input from their customers. They asked customers to tell them what could be done to improve existing products and inquired about what customers thought regarding new product ideas generated by the company. Capturing the voice of the customer and evaluating what customers said quickly became the dominant means of gathering product requirements for companies large and small.

The actual mechanisms for collecting the voice of the customer vary by company. Customer inputs can come from a variety of sources — primary sources such as one-on-one conversations or secondary inputs collected by other means. Many companies collect customer requests through their products, online communities, sales organizations, customer service databases, site visits, client conferences, user meetings, and a multitude of other sources. The range of possible data sources is quite large and it takes a concentrated effort to collect and organize the information into something that is coherent enough for you to use.

Once a process is established to identify and collect the various sources of available information, you must organize it so that priorities rise to the surface. This generally involves establishing a framework for prioritizing the various inputs. Once complete, you must take additional steps to ensure that as information is proactively collected, it is continually fed into a product decision framework for evaluation.

Although the initial stages of collecting and evaluating the available data from clients and across the organization is laborious, the information that results is often very useful. The data, filtered through a decision-making framework, will *quickly point to ways that your existing product line can be augmented.* Another important benefit of using a decision framework is that it provides you with a logical rationale for explaining why you have decided to invest in one product enhancement over another. Having a logical rationale to explain to both internal and external customers alike why you choose to invest in one area over another is tremendously helpful.

The voice of the customer approach offers another benefit as you step into your new role. It provides you with a means to improve your product from *readily available data sources.* This is important, as it is likely that the wheels of product development have continued to churn forward as you begin your product management role. It will take time for you to accumulate the necessary market information to confirm or alter the direction of your product. In the meantime, the inputs you collect and evaluate provide a means for you to make positive changes to your product without upsetting the existing momentum of the organization. As you collect more market data and make sense of it, you're then in a better position to support, with facts, any changes you think are required to achieve your product objectives.

There are limitations to this customer-driven approach. It relies heavily on the assumption that customers know exactly what they want, can communicate their needs in a clear and actionable manner, and will ultimately be willing to pay for the enhancement or product you create. Unfortunately, this is not always the case.

Also, keep in mind that the information you're receiving from customers is viewed from their perspective ("tree"), not from a wider market perspective ("forest"). Customers are often able to communicate known or *explicit* needs but are often unable to see the broader market needs. These unknown or unmet *latent* needs generally have to be identified through other mechanisms.

If you choose the customer-driven approach to pursuing your product management objectives, it's important to keep in mind the two different types of needs. As a product manager you're positioned better than your client base to spot latent needs. This is because latent needs are often more easily seen from the "forest" perspective. Your position grants you access to a wide range of information and enables you to see broader patterns in the market data, as opposed to the smaller set of information available to the individual customer. Given that customers are often better at communicating *their* explicit needs, it is important to reserve a quotient of your product development activities for what I call an *innovation reserve*. That is, incorporating a reserve in your development plan, say 20 percent, to invest in bringing to market capabilities that address perceived latent needs that your customers may be unaware that they have.

The strength of the voice of the customer approach lies in its ability to capitalize on the readily available sources of primary and secondary customer information — some of which already resides *inside* your organization. It also enables you to augment your existing product and preserve existing product development momentum while you gather the necessary market information with which to make informed decisions about your product's future direction.

The customer-driven approach of capturing the voice of the customer is well suited to augment existing products. Conversely, it is not as well suited for developing new innovations given its reliance on explicit needs.

WORKFLOW ANALYSIS

The phrase "workflow" is associated with business process re-engineering. It is used to describe the work processes used to arrive at a business objective (i.e., paying bills, managing benefits, or handling customer complaints). Your goal in conducting workflow analysis, as a product manager, is to gain deep insight into how your customers accomplish their work and correctly identify the problems they deal with so you can provide solutions.

BUSINESS PROCESS RE-ENGINEERING

Business process re-engineering (BPR) was launched in the 1990s to help organizations fundamentally rethink how to accomplish work tasks by looking at the processes and sub-processes that support the achievement of those tasks. The goal of BPR was to radically redesign a company's business processes to create increased efficiency. This was accomplished by eliminating tasks that added no value and aligning tasks across the functions, not solely within them. Business process re-engineering lost favor as it quickly became associated with downsizing efforts.

To gain this perspective, you must spend time with customers or prospects and map out their work process in great detail. This includes capturing the steps that are taken to achieve a desired outcome, the people involved, and their interactions. By conducting this analysis you're hoping to identify new ways to improve existing processes or introduce new product and service innovations that transform existing procedures and solve your customers' business issues.

As you conduct workflow analysis with different participants, it becomes possible to identify common business problems shared by a broad set of customers and prospects. These emerging patterns provide insight into larger market opportunities. The information you collect from these customer process mapping activities, coupled with your market knowledge, often provides opportunities to transform the way your customers accomplish their objectives.

You begin workflow analysis by documenting each step of a customer's workflow — the interactions between different people in a process, their productivity, and output — to establish a baseline. Once you have documented the baseline, you can find opportunities to reduce inefficiencies, save time, save money, and increase the satisfaction of those performing tasks as part of the business process.

New technologies and service capabilities often spur workflow process improvements. Excellent examples of this are found in the document and medical industries where digital capabilities have enabled significant improvements over the traditional paper-based processes. The ability to store documents electronically and move them from one point to another without physically having to transport them, increases efficiency and saves time and money.

Once you examine a business process in depth, opportunities often arise to take steps out of a process or identify an aspect of a process that is not being adequately served. Whether you're removing steps or completely transforming a process, the improved efficiencies that result often create a win-win scenario for both the customer and the company.

WHAT IS A BASELINE?

Simply put, a **baseline** is a starting or reference point established for the sake of future comparison to later data. Whether it is establishing a baseline to measure how your products are doing when you took responsibility for them, or how efficient your company's product development activities are, you'll find baseline information to be an important tool to help continually improve the performance of your product and demonstrate results.

Successfully implementing a workflow approach embeds you and your company in the daily mechanics of your client's business processes and results in a deeply intertwined and co-dependent relationship. The analysis you conducted into the way people interact in the workflow process gives you extremely valuable information that you can use to make your marketing and sales processes more effective. In essence, you know who you need to sell to, what problems they face, who interacts in the process, who the economic buyer is, and what each party in a process is looking for.

The workflow method is a powerful tool and is equally well suited to identifying opportunities to augment existing value or create new value through innovation.

Keep in mind that to successfully execute this approach in a market with well established business processes, you'll need a clear and compelling value proposition. Your insights must generate a significant enough return that both your organization and the client can profit from your value augmentation or creation activities to be worth the investment. Additionally, businesses tend to be cautious adopters of unknown or unproven companies' products or services.

Business processes are central to how companies generate revenue and profits so clients will want to make sure they're comfortable with your company before entering a relationship that creates a high level of co-dependence with the associated risks. Finally, the process of mapping customer business processes and identifying areas for market- or client-level innovation requires a significant amount of customer engagement and time.

OUTCOME-DRIVEN INNOVATION

The outcome-driven approach focuses on understanding what customers are trying to achieve as they do their jobs and the metrics they use to define success. This methodology was introduced in the book *What Customers Want* by Anthony Ulwick.[1] Its objective is to reduce the rate of failure associated with earlier product development methodologies. The outcome-driven method postulates that once you know what jobs customers are trying to accomplish and what outcomes they are trying to achieve, you're able to methodically create products and services that generate value.

To use this approach, you have to determine where you need to focus. Is it on the end user, the economic buyer, a partner, or someone else? The next question that must be answered is who in the value chain makes the most important judgments about value and the metrics used to define success? As part of this process it's important that you capture the measures of value that define how customers want to get the job done: the process steps taken, the outcomes they are striving to achieve, the definition of what it means to do the job perfectly, and the constraints that stand in the way of successfully completing the job. There are typically between 50 to 150 desired outcomes per job. You need to capture *all* of them to determine whether these needs are underserved or overserved. It is very important that these success criteria are defined by the customer, not *your* organization.

To collect this information, you will conduct a series of customer interviews that allow you to gather a statistically significant sample of the client base. As you aggregate the data, a set of performance metrics will emerge.

Once the data are in hand, you must score and then chart them on a graph that shows areas of opportunity. These areas fall into three categories of needs: underserved, overserved, and appropriately served. Underserved areas are opportunities for growth. Overserved areas are opportunities for ceasing investment, cost reduction, or potentially disruptive innovation.

One of the most significant benefits of this approach is its ability to reduce variation in the success or failure of value creation activities by offering a means to thoroughly understand what the customer's metrics of success are, *upfront* — in other words, *before* you invest in developing a product or extend a product's capabilities. This methodology is equally useful in augmenting the existing value of a product or creating new value through innovation. By identifying needs that are over- or underserved, you can effectively target the areas that give you the best chance of enabling your customer's success in a way that doesn't waste your resources and reduces variability in launching products.

This method requires a significant amount of customer engagement as you work closely with your clients to build up a statistically relevant sample. The collection of information is very structured and data that does not correspond to the framework is not considered later. In other words, you'll need to turn a blind eye to what customers tell you they want if it doesn't conform to the process you're following! It will also require a clear understanding of your company's objectives and may identify opportunities that have traditionally resided outside your company's expertise. This will raise thought-provoking questions.

THERE IS MORE THAN ONE WAY TO ACHIEVE YOUR OBJECTIVES

As you think back through the three product management approaches we just discussed, you can trace a continuing evolution in the way product managers refine their methods by attempting to reduce the chances that a product or set of product capabilities will not be successful in the market. Options exist that allow you to examine what customers are *telling you*, how they *accomplish their work*, and what they are *trying to achieve*. Selecting the right method will depend on what *your* organization is attempting to achieve, the relative maturity of the organization, the amount of time you have to achieve your objective, and the available skills and resources that you can draw upon.

CHAPTER THREE'S TIPS FOR TAKING CHARGE

- Your company's business plan is an ideal place to start getting up to speed on your market and product. It also allows you to see the world through the eyes of the author, most likely your CEO. Reading the business plan saves time and helps you begin adding value more quickly.

- Remember to take the cultural temperature of your organization *before* asking for access to the business plan. Not all organizational cultures will be open to sharing the plan in its entirety. If yours won't, consider asking for the part of the plan that relates directly to your area of responsibility. Regardless of the level of access you're granted, you'll need to keep any aspects of the plan that are shared confidential unless you're told otherwise. Establish the ground rules for who you can discuss the information with when you receive access.

- Product management is not one size fits all and your company's growth stage will have an impact on your role. At each stage of growth, emphasis is placed on the skills best suited to achieve a desired business objective. These business objectives are: creating new value through innovation, augmenting existing value, or a combination of both. Understanding your company's objectives will help you succeed.

- Product management methods are evolving and there is more than one way to achieve your product objectives. Choosing the best method to achieve your goals is predicated on knowing the range of available options, thoroughly understanding *your* company's business objectives, and assessing the amount of time and range of skills that are at your disposal.

CHAPTER FOUR: ESTABLISH FIRM FOOTING

The sound of a polite knock jolted me out of my stack of notes and back to the present. Looking up I saw Sheri, Sinclair's assistant, standing at the edge of my desk. I quickly checked the clock to see what time it was, worried that I was late for my second one-on-one meeting with Sinclair. Relieved to see there was still 20 minutes until my scheduled meeting, I mentally breathed a sigh of relief as I turned toward Sheri.

Before I could say a word, Sheri beat me to the punch. "Sorry to interrupt you Sean, but Sinclair is going to finish his phone call in about five minutes and he asked me to see if you could stop by a bit earlier. Are you available?" she inquired, knowing full well I was. "Of course Sheri," I responded. "See you in five minutes." With a friendly nod, Sheri departed as quietly as she had arrived.

I turned back to my desk and reached for the two copies of my freshly printed meeting agenda and the page of open questions. As I ordered the documents, I thought back to my last meeting with Sinclair. It had been our first one-on-one meeting since I accepted the position. During our initial meeting Sinclair had made it clear that he was glad I had taken the position. Then he handed me a copy of the business plan — all 28 pages of it. Once again, he reminded me that it was to be kept confidential and only discussed with members of the senior leadership team.

Sinclair had suggested I spend a significant amount of time with the document and come prepared for today's meeting with any questions I might have, as well as preliminary thoughts about my next steps. After reading the plan, I had taken the initiative to meet with each member of the senior leadership team to be sure I understood their perspectives of the business plan. The only person I had not been able to meet with face-to-face was my former boss Robert, our sales leader, who lived in another state and came into the office every two weeks. We had discussed the plan by phone. I was rereading my notes from these meetings when Sheri had knocked.

Glancing quickly at my computer's clock, I realized that I'd better leave my desk and make my way over to Sinclair's office or I was going to be late. Two minutes later it was my turn to announce myself at Sheri's desk, and I was quickly ushered into Sinclair's office. Sinclair was just finishing his call and motioned for me to sit at the table in his office. As he hung up, I pulled out two copies of the outline and waited for him to join me.

Sinclair exhaled. "Thanks for being flexible Sean," he said as he sat down. "I realized my call was going to end more quickly than I had anticipated..." After a couple of moments had passed, Sinclair changed gears and inquired, "So, have you found the business plan useful?" "Absolutely," I replied with conviction. Smiling faintly, Sinclair glanced at the outline I had handed him and nodded thoughtfully.

"Before we begin with your agenda topics, Sean, I would like to get a couple things out on the table," he stated. My curiosity piqued, I listened carefully for what Sinclair was going to reveal. Sinclair continued, "I have a lot of confidence in you Sean, which is why I asked you to take this position. Now that you've had time to absorb the business plan and talk to the functional leaders in the company, I'm sure you can see why your role is so important." Because I sensed there was something important coming, I tried not to let his compliment cloud my thinking.

"In fact, your role is so important to our future growth that I'm going to continue to have you report to me," he concluded. My mind was racing as I contemplated the impact of this decision. I found that I was both pleased and concerned! "Part of the reason for this reporting structure is that I do not want the other departments' functional goals to influence the decisions you're about to make," he continued. "I believe you need to look at the market facts objectively and not be unduly influenced by our short-term revenue goals, our sales and marketing activities, or our engineering efforts." Sinclair paused for a second so I could absorb the news. "I need you to think about our products, our profitability, and our market over the long-term."

"I recognize that this will create a certain degree of dynamic tension between your product objectives and the short-term objectives of the other areas of the business, but I believe it will lead to some *healthy* tension," he stated matter-of-factly. "I also believe that I'm best suited to balance these needs on behalf of the organization, and so I think it's best if you report to me for now." I nodded silently, thinking about my relationship with Robert, our Vice President of Sales. "I recognize that as a product manager you're not going to be able to keep everyone happy and that the decisions you're going to make are critically important to our future success. I want you to know that you have my full support. The reason I'm telling you this is I've been through all of this before, in my last company, and the path ahead will not be easy on you personally. Some of your relationships will change based on your new role. I just want you to be prepared."

As Sinclair finished talking I couldn't help but be impressed with his leadership

> ## VALUE PROPOSITION
>
> A **value proposition** is a marketing tool that makes a clear and concise statement about the tangible results a customer will receive from using your product or service. The ideal value proposition appeals to your customer's strongest decision-making criteria. These may include:
>
> - Decreased costs
> - Improved revenues
> - Increased market share
> - Enhanced operational efficiency
> - Better customer retention levels

skills and candor. I had started to see signs of the changing nature of my relationships with the sales team and others as I made my rounds to clarify aspects of the business plan. However, it had not fully dawned on me that the change in my role would change the nature of some of my working relationships. I guess I should have known.

Sinclair pulled me back into the moment with his next statement. "Before we dig into your agenda, I just want you to know I think you're taking the right initial steps to begin to add value in your new role. Identifying sources of information that can enhance your knowledge and decision-making capability is important. Keep it up. I follow a similar philosophy myself when I accept a challenge. One of my mentors used to say, *'Good generals make sure to secure their base of operations before expanding outward.'* In other words, keep collecting and processing the information that you need to make good decisions on behalf of the organization."

"Now, let's dive into that agenda of yours..."

BEGIN BY TAKING AN INVENTORY

Sean is well on his way to establishing firm footing and a solid base of knowledge. He still has a lot to learn and his approach of starting with the business plan to understand the original business assumptions has set him on the right path to formulating his own conclusions about the current state of the business and how he can best achieve his product objectives. Sean has also taken his own proactive step of reaching out to Sinclair's direct reports who also know the details of the plan, and this has helped him on two fronts. He has spent time learning their perspectives of the current state of the business, and they are now aware that he has been granted access to the business plan and Sinclair's confidence.

Understanding the baseline assumptions of the business is very useful. However, markets are not static. They continue to change, and the original business plan has probably not been updated since it was written, which in the case of Alpha Technology Ventures was over two years ago. So, it's very important that Sean rolls up his sleeves and begins meeting with customers while he seeks to pull together more current information. Let's examine and then talk through a list of internally available materials that can help Sean get a current view of the business situation.

INTERNAL SOURCES OF INFORMATION

- ☑ Market research
- ☑ Customer list
- ☑ Presentation materials currently in use
- ☑ Company collateral
- ☑ Win/loss analysis data
- ☑ Customer proposal template and signed contracts
- ☑ Available competitive information
- ☑ Customer data sources within the organization
- ☑ Defect reports
- ☑ Product cost information or a product P&L
- ☑ Existing product-related materials

MARKET RESEARCH

It is quite likely that your company has commissioned some market research. The term market research refers to an organized effort to collect information about markets or customers for the purpose of minimizing business risk. Research is often used to investigate new business opportunities, identify the cause of a business problem, or provide additional information to aid in making an important decision.

Most companies do not conduct market research themselves; they hire agencies or third parties. To ensure the success of the research project, your company assigns a business sponsor that works closely with the market research team to define the scope of the project, collect the necessary information, analyze the data, and interpret the information. Unless your company is one of the lucky few, research is generally outsourced because most companies do not find it cost effective to staff market researchers, although market research skills are often highly valued.

As a product manager, you'll likely commission market research yourself at some point in your career. Market research activities cover a wide variety of areas. Six of the more typical areas in which market research is conducted include:

- **Market information** — the size of the market, how it is segmented or current trends.

- **Market structure** — identifying the major players and their market share, brand market share, or the market's distribution structure.

- **Buyer perceptions** — buyer needs' assessment or perceptions of various brands and suppliers.

- **Product** — analysis of the available products, usage and consumption patterns, differentiation, segments served, or satisfaction levels.

- **New product development** — defining unsatisfied needs, product acceptance, or communication.

- **Pricing** — sensitivity, trends, or mapping existing pricing structures.

If you think back to the original business plan you'll see that some of the information that was in the plan could have come from market research. The best places to look for market research activity within your organization are with your CEO and your counterparts in marketing. Ask whether they have conducted any research either in support of the business plan or since. Because they may have sourced a research firm for your colleagues, your marketing team will likely be aware of anyone conducting market research.

Also inquire whether your company has commissioned a customer satisfaction survey. Most companies with a significant customer base start to monitor customer satisfaction. These surveys often probe customers on more than just how satisfied they are with your company; they also look at the key drivers of value or satisfaction with your product and can contain useful information that you need to be aware of as you move forward.

GET A LIST OF YOUR CUSTOMERS

Understanding who you're currently selling your products to will tell you a lot about your company and your product. Is the customer that is purchasing your product primarily made up of major accounts, or are you serving the needs of standalone organizations? Are you selling to executives or the end users? Are your products being integrated with other products or services to create a robust solution or do they stand on their own? The more you know about who you're selling to and the reasons why you're selling to them, the better.

There is no better way to see who currently values your product than to get from finance a descending dollar volume list of your active customers. If the list includes clients that have gone inactive and stopped using your product, even better!

Look closely at this list of active customers and look for patterns that emerge as you review it. What do the top 20 percent of customers have in common? How far-reaching are your products in terms of geography? Does the list contain resellers of your products or the end users? Investigate your observations with the sales, professional services, and customer service teams.

Now, look closely at the list of customers that stopped using your product. Do they share a common characteristic or does it appear random? Placing a call or arranging to stop by to visit customers that chose to drop your product can tell you a lot about what you need to do to improve your product in the future. Many former customers will be very open to discussing why they no longer use your product.

The data contained in this report can also be used, in combination with information you solicit from the sales team, as a means to pinpoint thought-leading customers who will help you enhance your product. And it can help you prioritize your time as you begin to move outside of the organization and interact directly with customers to learn more about how they are using your product.

Knowing who your most valued customers are becomes important as you begin to interact with the accounts that provide significant revenue to your organization. Take the time to identify and meet these customers once you're ready. Finally, this descending dollar report also serves as a handy reference as you begin to receive inbound calls from customers or special requests from the sales team.

KEEP CUSTOMER LISTS CONFIDENTIAL!

A list of your company's customers is an important organizational asset that must be treated confidentially. Customers provide the revenue your company counts on to grow and create new product or service capabilities. If your company ever comes up for sale, one of the key assets that potential acquirers will want to consider, to determine the value of your company, is the health and span of your company's customer base. Therefore, customer lists have a monetary value, and it is important for you to treat the list confidentially to ensure that it does not fall into the wrong hands.

COLLECT PRESENTATIONS

Now collect a sample of the customer-facing presentations currently in use across your organization. Sales, marketing, business development, professional services, and the executive team are all directly interacting with customers and presenting the company and your product. Collect the most current versions of these presentation materials from each functional area and compare them. How are they portraying your product? Is there one consistent representation of your product's value proposition or does each presentation portray the product differently? Do any of the presentations discuss future development activities? If so, what did the presentation promise down the road?

Depending on the size of the organization and its marketing sophistication, it's not uncommon to discover a wide range of presentations with an equally wide range of ways that your product is being positioned in the market. Knowing what is being said is the first step to gaining control of the message.

Alpha Technology Ventures is a perfect example. Sean was originally asked to become a product manager to help sort through the different product enhancement requests that came about as the company began to rapidly expand its customer base. Sinclair knew that without a central person managing the product and crafting a well-defined value proposition, the sales team would continue to make a wide variety of promises to clients regarding what the product would do *that conflicted with what it actually now did.* The lack of a well understood value proposition was creating problems further downstream. This resulted in a significant number of competing requests for additional product enhancements.

By carefully examining these presentations and what is being communicated to the market, you can quickly gain insight into how cohesive or fractured the message has become. It is also a great way to determine what, if any, customer commitments have been made that you'll either have to honor down the road or address. Presentations are often an excellent indicator of how large the challenge is in terms of managing the perceptions of your colleagues, the client base, and the market going forward.

COMPANY COLLATERAL AND MARKETING MATERIAL

Next, visit your marketing team and ask for copies of all the existing sales and marketing materials for your product. These can include company brochures, press releases, publications, articles, advertising, product fact sheets, white papers, case studies, webinar schedules, and the calendar for organized customer events. Once you've collected the materials, take a close look at the sales support materials. Do the product fact sheets, articles, white papers, case studies, and publications focus in on a consistent story about the value of your product? Or do they tell different stories?

Now look at the corporate marketing materials: the company brochure, press releases, and advertisements — are they in line with the story the sales organization is using? If all these elements are not aligned, you'll need to address this once you finish your analysis.

WIN/LOSS ANALYSIS DATA

Many organizations implement a process to analyze victories or defeats at the end of the sales process. The analysis itself is either handled by a sponsor inside the organization or by a third party. If the analysis is conducted internally, it's usually led by someone who is not directly involved in the sales process, such as a product manager, a marketing manager, or some other party that is well respected and relatively bias-free. The other option is to outsource this analysis to an objective third party that collects and analyzes the data on your organization's behalf. Regardless of who conducts the actual analysis, it's important that the data are collected in a manner that is not centered on assigning "fault," but rather viewed as a means of improving operational effectiveness.

The data that result from this analysis are often very helpful in gaining a current understanding of how your new customer or prospect perceives your product and your organization. The information that is collected can also assist the sales team by identifying ways they can improve their execution.

The person conducting the win/loss interview begins by reaching out to the unsuccessful sales prospect or newly acquired client to ask a series of questions that shed light on your company's interaction with their organization. The actual interview questions vary by company but the general framework flows something like this:

- What companies were involved in the selection process?
- How did we stack up?
- What did you perceive as our strengths and weaknesses?
- What did you perceive as the strengths of weaknesses of our competitors?
- What factors led to our victory or loss?
- Can you overview the decision-making process?
- Who was involved and what were the key selection criteria?
- What could we have done differently to improve? (Ask regardless of a win or a loss.)
- The interview often closes with an open-ended question to solicit any final thoughts.

The information that results from these interviews can be very insightful. Make sure to get your hands on the available data and talk to whoever is conducting the analysis to ensure that you get copies of the information as new reports come out. Understanding how your product is being perceived by prospects and new customers will give you additional insight into the market.

CUSTOMER AGREEMENTS AND SIGNED CONTRACTS

Another good way to gather information about your product is to go to your legal counsel and ask for several copies of recently signed customer agreements, as well as the proposal template that the sales team is using. Take a close look at the template and examine the standard language.

Now take a look at a recently signed contract. What changes were made? Did the pricing change? Perhaps the length of the agreement? Is there a cost of living adjustment in the contract or did it get removed? Were product or service components "thrown in" to close the deal? Did the language regarding press releases or referenceability get scratched out? Were contractual promises made to enhance the product? It's not unusual to see any combination of the above take on a legal life of their own in contracts.

Now look across all the contracts on your desk. Is there a pattern that you see emerging? If so, it might tell you something important about the way the sales organization perceives the value of your product (something you might not learn by talking to the sales team themselves)! It will also tell you something about how your customer perceives the value of your product. As they say in good detective work, follow the money. It generally leads you to something important!

AVAILABLE COMPETITIVE INFORMATION

Every organization collects information on their competition. The best places to source internally available competitive information are the sales team, the marketing team, and even your executive team. There is one thing to keep in mind as you collect competitive information — you should only use competitive information that is in the public domain.

The sales organization comes into contact with competitor information during the sales process, while attending conferences, and as they engage in other customer-centric activities. Sales teams routinely collect competitive information and share it with their sales counterparts in order to enhance their effectiveness. To make sure you have access to this material, talk to the sales team about getting on their distribution list as new competitive material makes the rounds. Also be sure to collect the most recent materials that are currently available.

Many marketing teams collect and aggregate competitive data into a central repository to make the material available to a broader audience. Your marketing team might also monitor the news wire for information about competitors and channel this information to appropriate parties in the organization. If so, you should ask to join the distribution list.

COST OF LIVING ADJUSTMENT

Cost of living adjustment (COLA) is an annual adjustment made to the price of an item to offset the impact of inflation over a specified time.

Let's walk through an example. Say that the rate of inflation over three years is 4 percent each year and that Alpha Technology Ventures is selling a three-year software subscription for $10,000 per year. Each year, the money that Alpha Technology Ventures would receive for their software subscription would decrease by the rate of inflation, 4 percent. Extended over the entire three-year contract, the compounded rate of inflation would seriously decrease what the company received for their product subscription. In other words, the price of the subscription would remain fixed at $10,000, but the actual dollars received each year would continue to decline over the life of the contract.

Additionally, the next time the company renewed the customer's subscription, the sales team would need to overcome the hole created by the three years of compounded inflation. Without a COLA clause in the contract, the customer would perceive the renewal price as significantly higher than it actually is — in terms of inflation-adjusted dollars. To be sure this doesn't happen, companies often add COLA clauses to customer agreements to make sure that the annual price received for a product keeps pace with the actual rate of inflation. This makes renewing existing agreements much easier.

But this approach can cut both ways, because it's possible for a market to have a negative inflation rate in a given year. Companies like Alpha Technology Ventures often include a COLA clause in their customer agreements to guard against this inflation risk. The actual index used to measure the rate of inflation varies based upon the industry being served.

The executive team also comes into contact with competitive information as they interact with customers and business partners. Most of this information is gleaned through peer-to-peer conversations as opposed to the documents that often come from sales and marketing. Still, the information collected by your organization's leadership team can be tremendously helpful in anticipating competitive threats or strategic moves.

As you collect competitive information from all the available sources, bear in mind that it is likely that your organization's future success is not hinged solely on what competitors are doing but on your understanding of your market and the things that you can do to capitalize on market opportunities. Most companies develop a superior market position by understanding their customers' needs better than anyone else.

> ## CAUTION! MISUSE OF COMPETITIVE INFORMATION CAN LEAD TO LEGAL LIABILITY
>
> There are significant legal risks associated with using confidential or proprietary information that is not in the public domain. To minimize this risk, before proceeding always ask yourself: will the use of this information subject either my organization or me to a potential lawsuit? Thankfully, most of the organizations you're likely to compete against leave a significant amount of competitive information in the public domain.

IDENTIFY INTERNAL CUSTOMER DATA SOURCES

Your organization is likely awash with customer information that has never been centralized. Collecting available data and analyzing it can be useful in bringing you up to speed. Investigate where databases of customer information are being kept within your organization. For example, your customer service team may keep a database of incoming customer support calls, the topic discussed, and the current status of the request.

The customer service team may also be managing online client discussion groups that allow you to collect feedback from clients in real time. If you can't participate in the online sessions, ask your colleagues to provide you with a summary of the discussion. The marketing team may be another source of useful information, as they are likely collecting information related to lead generation, trade shows, and customer conferences. Identifying these sources of information will broaden your knowledge about your product's customer base.

DEFECT OR "BUG" REPORTS

If your company is like Alpha Technology Ventures, it produces technology products and software applications. One of the natural by-products of technology are imbedded flaws in the design, called defects or bugs. Many of these defects are identified during the quality control process before the product's release to the market. However, some defects ultimately make it past the testing processes and are identified by customers. As your clients discover these defects, the information is reported to the sales team, customer service, or others inside your organization and redirected to a member of the engineering team who attempts to duplicate the reported problem. Once a defect is confirmed, a priority rating is assigned to the problem.

The ranking system generally mirrors the following framework:

- **Critical issue** — a defect that has a major negative impact on your product's performance and needs immediate intervention.

- **High priority** — a defect that prevents the effective use of your product.

- **Medium priority** — a bug that increases the degree of difficulty in successfully using your product, but work-arounds are available.

- **Low priority** — a problem that affects the use of your product but is only a minor inconvenience to the user.

Confirmed defects are usually accumulated on a report that is shared with the product team to determine which problems should be fixed and what is the appropriate timing. The engineering team generally owns and maintains these reports. To get a copy of the current report you'll need to visit with them. At this point on your learning curve, defect reports will not be your immediate priority. However, this report will provide a glimpse into the efficiency of your engineering team and the processes they're following to resolve known quality issues. And, it will help you identify *who* is currently making the call to deploy resources to fix prioritized issues. Look over the list and file it away for future reference; you'll likely become more actively involved in making resource decisions in the near future.

PRODUCT COST OR PROFIT AND LOSS INFORMATION

You'll also want to accumulate information regarding the financial health of your product. If your organization has put a product profit and loss statement in place, now is the time to get a copy. The finance team can provide you with a copy, but a better idea is to spend some time with them and have them walk you through the P&L. That way, they can answer any questions you have regarding terminology, the information rolled up into each line of the document, and what you should be paying attention to as you step into your new role. The finance team will be tremendously helpful to you as you begin managing the financial aspects of your new position.

Many organizations do not have product profit and loss statements in place. If yours has not yet taken the steps to do so, inquire if the finance team has calculated the cost structure of your products. Although you may find they haven't done so, simply asking the question may trigger a desire to in the near future. Determining the cost of your products is the first step to figuring out whether your products are profitable.

EXISTING PRODUCT-RELATED MATERIALS

One final suggestion before we move on to discuss the external data sources that will help you round out your growing understanding of your product: Don't forget to inquire if there are any current product management materials available! These could include product roadmaps, visioning documentation, product-level business cases, and product launch materials or any other product documentation that may already exist.

Just because you are the first *"official"* product manager within your organization does not mean that aspects of the job were being completely ignored. More often than not, *someone was doing elements of the job*, in addition to their own. If these materials do exist, it's important for you to collect them so you can better understand any existing expectations you may have inherited.

EXTERNAL INFORMATION SOURCES THAT MAY PROVE USEFUL

Now that you've successfully gathered information from your executive team, finance, legal, engineering, customer service, sales, and marketing, you have a more up-to-date view of the state of the business and any challenges that lie ahead. To round out this view, let's look at a couple of sources of information *outside of your organization* that can help you put the final pieces in place and begin developing a plan of action.

ANALYST REPORTS

Many industries are covered by analyst organizations. Industry analysts interview and survey a variety of market participants to glean information about trends, directional forecasts, and models. Typically, analysts focus on a single industry, although the firms that they belong to cover a variety of industry segments such as healthcare, technology, entertainment, etc.

ANALYST REPORTS ARE OFTEN EXPENSIVE!

This information is not free. In fact, it can be quite costly, easily exceeding $1,000 per report. So before ordering any industry reports, check with your marketing team and your senior leadership to see if anyone else has already purchased them. If you decide to purchase the report, others in your organization will be interested in the information; so be sure to distribute your knowledge.

Analysts accumulate information by talking to the vendors, investors, business partners, buyers, and users in a given industry. Interviews and surveys allow industry analysts to build a composite view of a particular market. The information that results from this detailed analysis is then commercialized in the form of client briefings, consulting, publishing, and public speaking.

If you are in an industry that is covered by an analyst organization, it's often worth the time and money to obtain and read copies of the reports on your industry. The reports will generally outline useful information detailing what the analyst believes the current trends are, the key players in the market, the business models in use, and the metrics used to measure success.

OTHER SOURCES OF PUBLICALLY AVAILABLE COMPETITOR INFORMATION

Earlier we talked about the competitor information that is channeled into your organization from sales, marketing, and your executive team. There are a few other sources of competitive information that are worth spending a little time on as well.

10-K report — Public and private companies over a certain size and with more than 500 shareholders must submit a 10-K report to the U.S. Securities and Exchange Commission (SEC) once a year. A 10-K report contains a detailed overview of a company's performance and it follows a set format:

- Business overview
- Risk factors
- Properties
- Legal proceedings
- Voting matters
- Market information
- Financial data (consolidated)
- Management discussion and analysis

10-K reports are different than the annual reports that you may be familiar with if you own stock in a company. The 10-K report is an official document that is required by the government. Most annual reports to shareholders are unofficial documents that are sent to shareholders when a company holds an annual meeting or is conducting a vote to elect directors.

Both types of documents are excellent sources of information regarding your competitors' market activities, areas of focus, and finances — although they are generally not light reading. You'll need to sort through a lot of detail to find useful information. Filed 10-K reports are available for free online in the SEC's Electronic Data Gathering, Analysis, and Retrieval system (EDGAR database).

Social media — Social media provides another source of valuable information to round out your understanding of what is being said about your product. The key to a successful online search is to find the blogs, discussion groups, and other settings where your customers and prospects are having meaningful conversations. Listen to what this audience is saying and hone in on the themes and identifiable trends. Pay close attention to who is actually having the conversation. Auditing these conversations can provide you with useful data on ways to improve your product.

Competitors' websites — Your competitor's websites often offer valuable information regarding products, industry announcements, and management presentations to shareholders. All of this information will further enhance your understanding of the competition.

INFORMALLY SURVEY YOUR INTERNAL CONSTITUENTS

You are now armed with a tremendous amount of information about your product. Take the time to analyze and absorb all the information. Based on what you learned, is your organization on track to meet its business objectives? Now overlay what you learned about your competitor's activities and what your customers are saying about your products. Has your company clearly established the market momentum that will allow it to keep growing? Or are there obstacles in the path to future growth?

At this point, you probably know more than anyone else in the organization about your product. You now have a comprehensive set of information, and most importantly facts, that will aid you when you begin to draft a product strategy and create an execution plan for your product.

INFLUENCE MAP REVISITED

Now is a good time to pull out that influence map you completed a couple chapters ago. Look at the list. Some, if not all, of the people on this map are good candidates to receive a copy of the survey. Be sure to ask the various functional leaders to participate as well. The survey process does not need to be formal; in fact, the more informal the better.

Before embarking on these next steps, it's helpful to conduct an informal survey of your counterparts. The reasons for doing this include flushing out your colleagues' expectations regarding your new role and capturing their perceptions about the current state of affairs. By conducting this survey, you'll gain insight into their expectations and today's product execution realities. Capturing this information now, before you begin to take action, will provide you and your organization with a means to measure your future progress.

Here are some questions to consider asking:

- What do you see as the biggest opportunity for our product in the next two months to a year?

- What do you see as the biggest opportunity for our product over the next two to five years?

- What do you see as the biggest challenge for our product in the next two months to a year?

- What do you see as the biggest challenge for our product in the next two to five years?

- What needs to be fixed or changed to position us to for the next step?

- Do you believe we currently have a clear and compelling vision for our product?

- If so, is our product strategy well communicated throughout the organization?

- Does our product roadmap enable achievement of our vision and support the business plan?

- Do you believe our current product initiatives are on track? If not, please explain.

- Do you believe product management's goals and objectives are well understood?

- What do you expect from the product management function? List the top three expectations.

- Is product management appropriately aligned with the other functions to best support achievement of the company's product objectives?

- Do you believe that your functional area has a "voice" in the product development process?

- Do you feel that product management has a thorough understanding of our customers' needs?

- Does product management have well understood processes and milestones?

- How effective are our current product development activities in achieving on-time, on-budget, and on-scope results?

(A preformatted version of this survey is available on my website www.ActuationConsulting. com for you to download at your convenience.)

There are various means to distribute surveys; regardless of which method you use, closely examine the tabulated results. The data will tell you a lot about what is working and what you'll need to pay attention to going forward. Share the information with your organization or at least those who participated in the survey. They will likely find the results insightful and appreciate seeing what others think. With the results of the survey in hand, you now have a baseline with which to measure your future progress.

SAVE THAT SURVEY!

Hold onto that survey you just distributed. You'll likely want to send it around one more time to measure your progress later in the year. As we proceed, we will discuss more quantifiable measures of success that you'll use instead of the survey. But implementing those tools will take time, and the survey will give you a means of measuring your progress in the meantime.

DEVELOPING A PRELIMINARY PLAN (HYPOTHESIS)

It is now time to give some thought to all that you've learned. I often find it helpful to go offsite, where I won't be interrupted, and begin to think about my future plan of action. Your objective at this stage is to rough out a hypothesis of where you want to take your products based on the information you've collected and the preliminary conclusions you've drawn from your analysis. Remember, you're simply drafting a preliminary version of your future action plan to "bounce off" various thought leaders in your organization and then test on some of your key clients and prospects. Putting it onto paper, even if it is virtual paper, is the first step to making your vision a reality.

Begin by drawing on the knowledge that you brought into your role and what you've since learned from your company's business plan. Then layer in the recently acquired intelligence you gained by meeting with customers, absorbing industry analyst reports, competitors' annual and 10-K reports, market research, and customer satisfaction surveys. Don't forget to include the information gathered from the internal survey you just conducted! Now think about what you learned from the other available internal data you collected. Taken together, you likely have enough information to sense the direction of where the market is headed and where your company is currently positioned. This knowledge will provide firm footing for you to think strategically and enable you to rough out a draft product strategy.

Your preliminary product strategy will reside on one presentation slide. Start by selecting a point on the horizon, say three years. Now settle on a starting point, say the end of this year. If your horizon point is three years and your starting point is year-end, you'll need to show customers what happens at the mid-point of this journey. In other words, the slide you're drafting will list strategic product milestones reflecting where you want to have your products at the end of the year, the mid-point, and in three years. Remember, these are not requirements but strategic milestones that you'll need to cross on the journey to attaining your market vision.

It is often easiest to start listing the key deliverables that are components of this strategy, beginning with the end of the current year since it is easiest to envision. Map out what you think this will *realistically* look like.

The next step is to lay out what you want things to look like in three years. Imagine what your products should look like in three years based on what you know about your market, the trends, and the competition. Now, what activities need to happen between where you are now and the three-year point? These strategy enablers end up in the mid-point bracket.

FIGURE 4. TEMPLATE FOR FRAMING A PRODUCT VISION

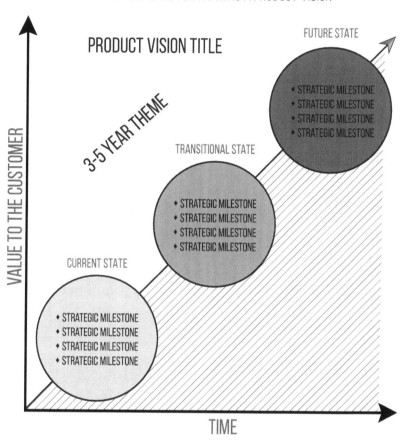

BE REALISTIC!

It's important that the current period in your product strategy *accurately reflects where your product is going to be at the end of the year.* If the information reflected in the current state is either inaccurate or unattainable, your customers will likely know that, and this will undermine their faith in your vision as it progresses. Product strategies by their very nature are aspirational but they also need to be tethered to reality!

IT TAKES TIME TO HONE A COMPELLING PRODUCT STRATEGY

This exercise is more difficult than it may seem. It is often easier to produce a lot of material or something that is complex than something as seemingly simple as putting a three-year directional vision with strategic milestones on a single piece of paper. Getting a completed draft roughed out can take one day or several weeks. If you get hung up, reach out to a friendly thought leader in your organization and ask them to help you round out what you've already accomplished.

Once you have a completed sketch of this desired future state in hand, it is time to call together thought leaders inside your organization and facilitate a brainstorming session to capture their views of the market as well. For now, our goal is simply to map out your product vision of the future and the strategy that will make or keep you a market leader.

CHAPTER FOUR'S TIPS FOR TAKING CHARGE

- Knowing more about your product line than anyone else in your organization will create the firm footing needed to make good decisions and enable you to step into a leadership role. Seeking out relevant information, in a well-organized manner, will allow you to rapidly develop a comprehensive view of the *current* state of your product.

- There is a tremendous amount of information about your product, your market, and your competitors at your disposal *inside* your organization — if you know where to look. Take the time to collect these materials and process the information.

- External sources of information are also available but may take longer to analyze. Be sure to acquire analyst reports, annual and 10-K reports, and publically available shareholder presentations from competing organizations and scour competitors' websites. The combination of internally available information, data gathered from your meetings with customers, and external intelligence will round out your view and enable you to start charting the course of your products.

- With an expanded knowledge base, you're now in a position to begin formulating a draft vision of where you think your products need to go to achieve or maintain a market leadership position. Use the information you collected to draft your *preliminary* hypothesis and capture the strategic milestones in a one-page document. This will set the stage for you to begin bouncing your product strategy off thought leaders within your organization and pressure test your vision.

CHAPTER FIVE: FORMULATE A WINNING APPROACH TO THE MARKET

Robert Lamp was perched at my desk. I wasn't surprised to find him waiting for me; I'd been anticipating this conversation ever since I had accepted the product management position. In my previous job, supporting the sales organization, Robert and I had enjoyed a strong working relationship. I hoped that my role change would not adversely impact our rapport. However, Sinclair had forewarned me that a change in our relationship was natural and to be expected.

Lunch in hand, I took a deep breath and tried to relax and not let my concern show. Robert was engrossed in email as I approached. As I drew closer, the sound of my footsteps alerted him to my arrival. He looked up and hurriedly pecked out a response to the email he had been reading. I chuckled to myself as I walked over to my desk; it often seemed like that mobile device was permanently stitched to Robert's hand. I couldn't help but think that the poor worn out device must be struggling to break free from the constant use but it was never able to make it any farther than his pocket!

With a knowing smile, and a mischievous twinkle in his eye, Robert opened the conversation. "So, I heard the news," he anted up. I wasn't sure which piece of news he was referring to, so I smiled defensively. As I reached my desk I set down my carne asada burrito knowing it would be cold before I had a chance to take a bite.

"Hi Robert," I responded cautiously, pretending I didn't hear him. "How was the trip in?" Robert smiled, the twinkle firmly etched into his eye. "Uneventful," he responded, savoring the chance to tease me and sensing my uncertainty. Determined to flesh out what he was after, I asked, "so what brings you to my desk? Isn't Sinclair's bi-weekly staff meeting going on?" Robert unconsciously patted the pocket that held his captive mobile device before responding. "Sinclair had to take a call from Kevin Knowles, so we won't resume the meeting 'til 1:00. You *know* Kevin don't you?" he added with the spark in his eye dancing devilishly.

I was beginning to suspect what brought Robert to my desk. The tip off was the rapidly flickering sparkle in his eye. Plunging ahead, I decided I would see if I could get to the root of his opening question. "I know who he is Robert, but I've never met him." "So, is the news you're referring to related to my presentation to the board at the annual management team review?" I probed. I tried not to flinch as I asked the question. The annual review was never far from my mind. I still had the better part of a year to get ready and I was painfully aware that I was not yet prepared for that critical meeting.

Robert didn't attempt to hide his satisfaction at the thought of my inclusion in the annual review. He was aware of the unease it was sure to generate since I had never interacted with the board before. Stepping up his teasing, he added, "Well, you'll get to know Kevin pretty well by the time the meeting's over." A smile like a Cheshire cat's burst across his face.

Having confirmed at least part of the reason why Robert was perched at my desk, I tried to rise above the angst the thought of the board meeting gave me. Looking Robert in the eye, I said, "I look forward to meeting him." The gleam in Robert's eye receded somewhat. I guess I sounded more confident than I felt.

Now that I'd effectively warded off Robert's good natured opening salvo, he decided to escalate. "First an invite to the management team review with the board and now reporting to Sinclair directly; you're quickly moving up in the world, Sean!" I looked around to see if I could find a fire hose. Robert needed a good dousing; he was clearly here to stir up my anxiety. Unfortunately there wasn't one within reach.

"Funny, it doesn't feel that way, Robert," I replied honestly. "Although I think it is fair to say that things have been moving along quickly since I took this role. By the way Robert, thanks for supporting my transition from your team to this new position. I never had a chance to tell you face to face," I added. "Happy to do it, Sean," Robert replied. "Just remember you *owe* me one." I had to smile at his response; Robert was always looking for an angle!

"So how has the transition been?" he asked, seemingly serious for the first time. Heartened by his apparent sincerity, I replied, "Sinclair has been really supportive and I've been working to collect information so I can become more effective. Based on what I've learned so far, I feel pretty confident that I can steer the products to where they need to go. Sinclair told me he's going to hold me accountable for keeping an eye on the market, our customers, and our profitability over the long term. The hardest part has been making the transition from doing things in real-time to thinking about things over a longer timeline."

Robert looked at me appraisingly, as if he was seeing me for the first time, and I could not read his thoughts. I had always been able to sense the direction of his thinking, but he seemed both open and closed as I tried to sense what was going on in his mind. Sinclair's warning continued to ring true as I waited on Robert's response.

"Well, it seems like Sinclair made a good choice, Sean," Robert said matter-of-factly. "I would never have imagined you could have changed this much in so short a time. Just remember that I'll be counting on you to make changes to our product as needed. Don't forget that you're a sales professional at heart." Sensing that a page had turned in the chapter of our relationship, I decided not to respond. I knew full well that everything would not go exactly as Robert wanted going forward. I was going to have to strike a balance between our short- and longer-term objectives, per Sinclair's directive.

As Robert reached into his pocket to stop his mobile device's incessant vibration, he smiled and said, "Sean, don't forget what it was like to be in sales. *You were once coin-operated too,*" he reminded me with a wink as he turned and headed back to Sinclair's meeting.

Alone with my cold lunch, I was fully aware that I had just left the sales roost and was now charting a new course in both my role and my career. There was no going back now, only forward.

As I contemplated my next step, I took a bite out of my burrito and opened the magazine that had come in today's mail.

Lost in thought, I mechanically flipped through the pages until I reached page 7. What stopped me at page 7? It was a quote from the hockey player Wayne Gretzky that seemed to sum up my next task as a product manager: *"Skate to where the puck is going to be, not where it has been."*

With a new found sense of clarity I finished my lunch and pulled out my draft product strategy.

DEVELOP A PRODUCT STRATEGY FOR YOUR OFFERING

The art of creating an effective product strategy is revealed in Wayne Gretzky's quote. To create an effective product strategy you must be able to anticipate shifts in your marketplace *before* they happen, and then position your product to capitalize on the emerging opportunity. Remember, creating a product strategy is not an exact science but it does need to be directionally correct. You're steering your product toward a point on the horizon and you'll be able to make incremental course corrections along the way.

In the last chapter, you learned how to find mission-critical information. The data we collected provided the necessary knowledge base to begin to draft a hypothesis that frames where you believe your product needs to go in the future. You also put your thoughts on a single slide based upon the format included in Figure 4. Before we take the next step, we need to make sure that your slide is ready. Let's look at what Sean did with his draft product strategy and compare it with what you've done.

FIGURE 5. A FINAL DRAFT OF ALPHA TECHNOLOGY VENTURE'S PRODUCT STRATEGY

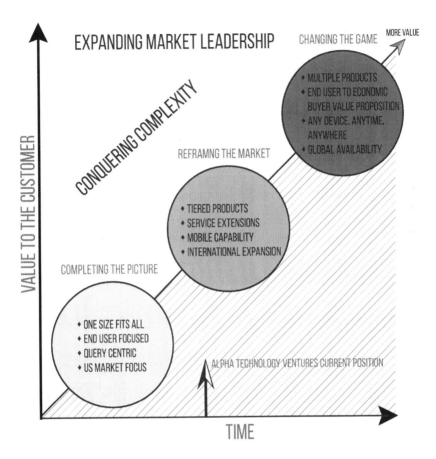

As you can see in Figure 5, Sean has finished his draft version of Alpha Technology Ventures product strategy. Notice the heading, "Expanding Market Leadership." This highlights Sean's overall product strategy: to increase the number of customers while lengthening the distance between Alpha Technology Ventures and its competitors. It also implies that Sean's product is *already* a market leader.

Also note that the left axis reads "Value to the Customer" and the bottom axis indicates "Time." The diagram indicates that over a specified period of time, typically three to five years, customer value will continue to increase as the company invests in Sean's product strategy. You can also see an arrow that runs at an incline from the bottom left corner to the top right. At the top of this line, Sean inserted a title to indicate that this product strategy will result in "more value" with which to attract more customers.

Each of the three time periods (represented by circles) has its own heading and a series of supporting bullet points. Notice that each heading is connected and supports Sean's theme of "expanding market leadership." It begins with completing the picture, talks about reframing the market, and then moves toward changing the game. Sean clearly strives to "own" the market and sees three distinct stages that his product will have to pass through to attain his market objective.

The first area, "Completing the Picture," attempts to accurately describe what the current state will look like at the end of this year. Sean is indicating that he has the core functionality in place to continue to grow, but needs to augment his existing product to fulfill its market potential. The supporting bullets list the key strategic product elements that are to be achieved by the end of the year in support of "completing the picture."

The second segment of the product strategy, "Reframing the Market," is focused on both the product and service capabilities that Sean believes will change the way that customers think about his product. Each supporting bullet point describes what customers can expect to see at the mid-point of this journey toward achieving the product strategy. These additional product and service capabilities expand the value of the product and serve as a *bridge* to the envisioned future state.

The final segment, representing attainment of Sean's product strategy, is entitled "Changing the Game." Sean clearly believes that the combination of the preceding investments and the final capabilities, captured in bullet points, give him the ability to change the nature of the way the game is played in the market in order to firmly establish his product as the market leader. Sean understands that market leaders generally dictate the rules.

Now that we have seen what Sean did with his draft product strategy, how does yours compare? If it needs fine-tuning, now is the time to do it. Your draft slide will most likely look very different than Sean's because the value created by your product or service is different than those of Alpha Technology Ventures. Capturing what makes your company different and ultimately successful, now and in the future, is the essence of creating a compelling product strategy.

If you're ready to move onto the next step, let's push forward.

ASSEMBLE YOUR COMPANY'S THOUGHT LEADERS

Now that you have a completed draft of your product strategy in hand, it is time to assemble thought leaders from within your organization to challenge your logic and refine your draft. Who are the thought leaders? They are forward-thinking individuals who can see the big picture, have a significant amount of domain knowledge, and frequently interact with customers. You might find your company's thought leaders in a range of roles, including a founder, professional services, research and development, marketing, or in sales leadership. You want to draw together the sharpest minds available in one room to help you forecast the direction of the market and challenge existing assumptions about your product. Make sure you schedule at least two to three hours for the meeting.

> **PLAN A MEETING WITH THOUGHT LEADERS WELL IN ADVANCE; THEIR TIME IS VALUABLE!**
> Remember, thought leaders are generally people with busy calendars. Make sure to book the meeting well in advance, ensure the projection equipment works properly, and be prepared to adjust your plan if someone drops out due to a scheduling conflict.

Before you meet with your company's thought leaders, send every attendee an explanation of your meeting objective and a copy of your product strategy. Make sure the product strategy is marked "draft" in big letters! By doing so, you'll be able to optimize the time during the meeting. Distributing materials in advance will provide everyone time to absorb the work you've done and come better prepared for the discussion.

Use the draft you created as a spring board to facilitate the discussion. Open the conversation by reminding everyone about your objective for the meeting and answer any questions that might come up before diving into the material. Begin by having the group focus on the current period. This is the easiest to see, so starting here will allow you to generate some meeting momentum.

As the team begins to react to your draft, capture their comments in bullets on the slide. You'll find that certain individuals will naturally dominate aspects of the conversation, so you'll need to make sure you keep everyone involved. If someone is not contributing, ask them what they think and give them a forum for voicing their opinion. Once you have the current period's suggested changes captured, move out to the most distant point on the time horizon.

Envisioning this future state generally leads to some great discussions. Make sure to capture what is being discussed, and if someone seems to have a particularly clear view of an element of the future, make note of who it was. You may find that you want to follow up with them after the meeting. I generally try to capture all the ideas in true brainstorming fashion and then have the group discuss and prioritize the ones that support the overall strategic theme. Remember Sean's theme of "expanding market leadership"? You'll generally find that there are more ideas than are feasible, so prioritizing is essential.

Now focus the group on the midpoint in the timeline. This transitional state to achieving your strategy is often the most difficult to capture because it requires linking the current state to the future. It often happens that items originally suggested for either the current state or the future make their way into this segment as the strategy starts to take shape.

WHAT IS BRAINSTORMING?

Brainstorming is an idea-generating technique used by teams to spark creative thinking. The members of a group gather in a central location and generate ideas; nothing is too far-fetched to be considered. Once the group's ideas have been captured, they are evaluated for usefulness. Brainstorming can be particularly helpful in identifying creative solutions to problems that have resisted traditional problem-solving methods.

Once the group has completed this exercise, you'll likely find that they are excited about having a tangible product strategy, and they'll likely ask for copies of your slide. Remind the group that you'll need to refine the work that was accomplished during the meeting and that you may need to follow up with them individually after the meeting is over to clarify any hazy points. Also let them know that as a next step, you'll be setting up time with some clients to solicit their input before the product strategy becomes "official."

After the meeting is over, spend time refining the wording and make sure that you fully understand all the concepts that you've included in the final draft. During the meeting you were busy facilitating and capturing ideas. You may find that your initial wording does not accurately express the concept you were attempting to capture. Look back to see who generated the original idea and follow up with them to see if you can nail down the best term. Refine the slide until you're happy with the outcome.

Once you're satisfied, take a second to reflect on what you've accomplished! You now possess a three- to five-year product strategy that resulted from your ever-increasing understanding of your product, your competitors, and the market. You've also been able to draw upon the support of your company's thought leaders to challenge your assumptions and help further refine your vision.

By collaborating with your company's influential thought leaders, you've no doubt ended up with a better result. They are now likely to help you champion this strategy inside and outside of the organization. No small accomplishment! Additionally, the product strategy framework you're putting into place will help align your team's future operational activities and ensure that the team stays within the boundaries of your product strategy. Most importantly, you've demonstrated leadership by setting the direction of your product.

KEEP PRODUCT STRATEGY OUT OF THE PUBLIC DOMAIN!

When you were researching competitors you did not find their product strategy in the public domain. To keep your product strategy from falling into the wrong hands, you'll need to construct a policy about who is going to be granted possession of this strategy slide. I generally restrict this to only the product manager who owns the product strategy and members of the executive team with the understanding that it will *never be left behind with clients, business partners, or other members of the organization.* The inherent danger is that if your competitors know your strategy they can beat you to the spot you're attempting to get to or negate any advantages you were hoping to accrue by implementing your vision. Distributing this slide can yield risks that are higher than the possible rewards. Mark it confidential and keep it close to your vest.

TEST ON THOUGHT-LEADING CUSTOMERS AND PROSPECTS

You're now able to meet with some key customers and prospects to see if they react as positively as you believe they will to your aspirational product vision. Pull out the customer list you collected earlier and reach out to members of the sales team or several of the thought leaders you worked with while refining your product strategy. Ask them who they believe the thought leaders are in the customer base. Once you have a list of thought-leading clients, set up a number of meetings, preferably face-to-face, to share your vision and ask for their input. Do the same with a smaller number of prospects. It is best if you take these clients out to lunch to develop a relationship with them and eliminate the risk of interruptions, but a more formal meeting will work as well. If a physical meeting is not possible, an online meeting is the next best option.

During these client meetings, explain your objective and ask the client where they believe the market is headed. Have them describe the top three business challenges they are facing today and how they are handling them. Be sure to capture their comments. Then explain that you're finalizing your thoughts regarding the future direction of your product and that you've developed a directional plan that you want to share with them and get their feedback. Let them know who pointed you to the client (or prospect) and explain that you're looking to engage with thought leaders to challenge your thinking. Then walk the client through your slide while reiterating that you would like them to challenge your logic.

After revealing the directional plan, assess the customer's reaction. Did the product strategy address any of the top three business challenges the customer told you about? Did they seem engaged and interested in your vision? Were they asking how they could contribute to making it a reality by investing time or money? Or did the product strategy you created not generate the reaction you expected? After conducting this test on a number of thought-leading customers, you'll have a good read on whether customers want to join you on the journey to attaining your strategy.

After meeting with customers, do a gut check. Do you feel more confident in your plan? Or do you need to make some adjustments? More times than not you'll find that the rigorous steps you took before sharing your product strategy with customers will have served you well and you'll be able to move past this stage and begin developing a supporting business case to justify future investments.

If you're confident in your plan and decide to press forward, you'll need to fine-tune this rolling product strategy as market conditions change; once a year is usually enough. With a strong strategy you'll be able to effectively align your annual execution plan with the product strategy you're pursuing. This will help keep your team's product efforts focused and reduce the chances that you'll dilute your resources by pursuing product development opportunities that are not aligned with your core vision and objectives.

WHEN VISITING CLIENTS, ALWAYS INVITE THE SALESPERSON RESPONSIBLE FOR THE ACCOUNT!

To maintain the strongest possible working relationship with the sales team, you should always invite the sales representative for the account you're about to visit to join the meeting. This will help your company on several fronts. First, you'll increase the trust between yourself and the salesperson. Second, information gleaned from the meeting may help the salesperson establish a stronger relationship with the client and ultimately lead to increased revenue opportunities for your business. Finally, the salesperson is ultimately responsible for managing the client relationship and it is good policy to include them in the conversation. The salesperson may choose not to join you, but including them will pay positive dividends.

DEFINE EACH MILESTONE

Now that you've spent time with thought leaders inside and outside your organization testing your product strategy and making any required adjustments, you're ready to take the next step. This involves focusing on the bullet points in your strategy slide and further defining what each element means.

During the earlier stages of defining your product strategy, you focused on *capturing the concept* in as few words as possible in order to summarize the meaning of each bullet. This approach allowed you to frame a compelling strategy on one slide. As you met with customers you had to explain each concept, using your own words, and you may have noticed that clients asked you for more detail to better understand the actual meaning of the concept you were communicating. You may also have noticed that as you met with each customer, your communication of the concept got crisper as you learned from each interaction how best to phrase the concept so it resonated with your clients.

With these interactions fresh in your mind, now is the ideal time to further define each concept. To accomplish this you'll need to pull together several short paragraphs that describe the substance behind the concept.

While it will take time to define what each of these milestones means, the energy spent will be worth the effort. Keep in mind that over time you'll be interacting with broader audiences made up of individuals at various levels of your organization as well as those of your clients. You'll want to make sure that these constituents can easily understand the scope of your strategy. Taking the time to flesh out each of these conceptual milestones will enable everyone in your organization, regardless of level, to receive the same message, and help you manage client expectations. Without further defining these milestones, you risk incorrect interpretations of your strategy taking on a life of their own and exceeding the original scope of your vision.

The result of your effort will be contained on a one-page document that further describes the concept, the value to the client, and any operational considerations that need to be taken into account before the eventual development of *each milestone*. Your presentation slide detailing each milestone should include several elements:

- Title and description of the milestone

- The customer value proposition

- Operational considerations

- The date the slide was created

Open each slide with the name of the milestone you're detailing. Then focus on creating a short paragraph that crisply describes, in as few words as possible, the substance behind the conceptual milestone. For example, if the milestone was "public accountability reporting," you might write: *Public accountability reporting will provide relevant executive-level summary information and trends at-a-glance in real-time to support governance and public reporting mandates.* If you know the information and trends, list them.

Next, construct the value proposition outlining why your customer should be interested in the capability you're planning to bring to market. Your value proposition should read something like this: *Alpha Technology Ventures' real-time public reporting capability will enable executives to review and effectively comply with mission-critical governance and public reporting mandates and reduce the risk of incurring a legal liability by 50 percent.*

Then lay out any operational considerations that need to be understood before attaining this milestone. Examples of things to consider might include developing a new wrap-around service offering, capital equipment purchases, educating channel partners on your new product capabilities, and increasing support staff.

Finally, make sure that you have a date on the slide for version control purposes. Because some of the elements you're defining occur later on, you may want to revise the initial draft as you get closer to the effective implementation date of the milestone.

Don't hesitate to reach back to the thought leaders who helped you refine the concepts in your product strategy. They will often be willing to help you review the accuracy of your expanded descriptions, particularly those that they may have contributed.

With the slides that support your strategy complete, you're now moving from developing a product strategy to beginning to execute your plan.

JUSTIFY WITH A SOLID BUSINESS CASE

Business cases are analytic tools requested by senior executives to ensure there is sufficient financial justification to invest in a market opportunity or a business problem's resolution. Depending on the scope of your product strategy and the expectations of your senior leadership team, you may or may not have to write a business case. Many organizations simply allocate a fixed number of resources to each product and expect you to manage the way the resources are used. Other organizations will require a cost benefit analysis justifying investments as a matter of course.

Regardless of how your organization operates, you'll find that you need a business case if you're proposing more than just enhancing the existing functionality of your product. Perhaps you're developing a tiered product strategy as part of your vision and you want to build out other product offerings and garner increased market share. Or maybe you're proposing developing a wrap-around service offering to augment the results your product provides to customers. Each of these scenarios is moving your product into new territory and will likely require you to justify the investment.

TIERED PRODUCT STRATEGY

Tiering refers to creating differentiated capabilities for your product that allow you to attract a greater share of the market than you might have been able to with a single product. Companies tier products by identifying a characteristic or set of characteristics that enables them to offer various degrees of value at different price points. Common tiering mechanisms include usage, functionality, construction materials, customer support, or bundled professional services. By tiering your products, you're able to increase the reach of your offering and attract customers who would not ordinarily purchase your core product.

What exactly is a business case? A business case is a fact-based and well thought-out proposal advocating a particular course of action to improve business performance or results. Business cases are usually developed by a product manager or another business sponsor to help executive decision-makers understand *why* a financial investment is required and what capability will result from the investment. The business case details the various benefits, costs, and risks of pursuing a suggested course of action and supports the request for a budget to enable the effort to proceed. Each company develops its own cultural framework for determining the type of information and financial thresholds needed to justify a successful business case. Let's take a closer look at the elements that are usually included:

- **Executive summary** — An executive summary is a consolidation of the most important information in your business case analysis. It makes the case for your proposed investment in clear and concise terms. The consolidated format enables a busy executive to take in the most important information at a glance, as opposed to wading through the detail contained in the rest of the document. The summary will generally be between one to three pages. It is the last section you'll write, since the information contained in the other sections of the business case provides the content for the summary.

- **Problem or opportunity statement** — The problem or opportunity statement section provides the necessary context to understand your request for additional resources. Make sure that your request for resources is aligned with your company's overall business strategy or it will have little chance of being successful. Clearly point out what is happening *today* that provides an opportunity for you to capitalize on. For example, you may have identified new market niches that are underserved or a means to improve your product's market performance by adding services.

- **Solution overview** — The solution overview provides a high-level description of the desired outcome. Explain how your proposed solution addresses the market opportunity or problem that you just highlighted.

- **Range of alternatives considered** — You'll need to review the alternatives you considered before selecting your preferred option. Outline the available options, *including doing nothing*. Describe why you selected the preferred option — why it rose to the surface. By taking the time to show that you evaluated all the available options, you'll demonstrate that you've given due consideration to the solution you're promoting.

- **Cost estimates** — After listing the available options, outline the estimated costs of pursuing your preferred course of action. You'll need to outline the total projected cost and the future financial return on investment. Make sure that the budget numbers you include can be justified and are as accurate as possible. In the case of Alpha Technology Ventures, the costs might include the full-time equivalents (FTEs) associated with the product teams' activities, product development costs, quality assurance and testing, and ongoing maintenance and administrative overhead.

WHAT IS AN FTE?

Full-time equivalents (FTEs) are a budgeting unit of measure. FTEs are calculated by combining the total number of full- and part-time employees assigned to a project, department, or organization to equate it to the number of full-time positions. One FTE equals 2,080 hours and can be broken down into fractions for accounting purposes. FTEs are often used to measure employee productivity or involvement in specific activities, for example product development or designated projects.

- **Benefit analysis** — Outline the expected benefits next. Your goal in this section is to compare the estimated costs with the benefits to assure your leadership team that the investment is worthwhile. The projected financial return needs to exceed the anticipated costs and any financial hurdles your company uses to justify an investment. Your executive team will be paying close attention to the rate of the anticipated return as well as the timing. Will the return happen within 12 to 18 months or will it take longer? Although the financial benefits will likely be the focus of the conversation, other benefits also matter. Be sure to capture all known benefits including increased market share, increased customer satisfaction, decreased employee turnover, etc.

- **Implementation timetable** — Your business case also needs to outline the implementation timetable and key milestones. You'll need to address how long it will take to bring your new capabilities to market and discuss what resources will be required to make it happen. Be sure to clearly communicate what you see as the major milestones and any dependencies.

- **Critical assumptions and risks** — You'll also need to outline identified risks and assumptions. What are the main risks that threaten the success of your endeavor? What assumptions have you made as you developed the business case? Be honest about these risks and assumptions.

- **Conclusion and final recommendations** — Finally, you'll lay out your conclusion and recommendation. Summarize your key themes as well as the benefits and the anticipated financial return. You likely have a sense of urgency; make sure it comes through in this section and propose next steps.

Your business case has now helped you align the executive leadership team behind your product vision, and you're one step further down the path to execution. At each step along the way you've built momentum and enlisted more support from different components of your organization. You've aligned thought leaders, key customers and prospects, and your leadership team behind your strategy. Now it's time to reach out and broadcast your message even further and engage with the people who will help make your vision a reality.

> ### BREAK-EVEN TIMEFRAMES VARY BASED ON THE TYPE OF MARKET YOU'RE IN!
> A common mistake many organizations make is to assume that there is a standard payback period — generally one year — on *any* investment in a new product. In existing markets, where you fully understand the market dynamics and who you're selling to, a 12- to 18-month payback period generally holds true. However, if you're launching a product into a new market, where you're learning about an emerging market's dynamics as you go, it can take up to five years to see a return on your investment!

VEST YOUR ORGANIZATION

Most of your time has been spent developing your strategy and enlisting the support of internal thought leaders, important customers and prospects, and your executive team. It's now time to begin vesting other team members inside your organization. The best way to achieve this is to create forums to share your product strategy and the high-level supporting detail that you created after meeting with customers.

During the influence map exercise, you identified the people who were both critical and important to your success. It's now time to meet with any of those team members who are not yet aware of your vision and spend some time bringing them up to speed. If you have direct reports that are unaware of your vision, start with them and work your way out to the other parties inside the organization. Some of these meetings will no doubt be one-on-one. For others, it might be more practical to choose a team or broader meeting. Regardless of your preferred approach, take the time to reach out to the people who support your product across every operational area of the business. It's important that the individuals that will be supporting your future efforts are fully vested in the direction you're taking them. This is not to say that everyone will agree with your plan.

RATES OF ADAPTING TO CHANGE VARY

Change can be extremely beneficial, but it can also produce stress. Your colleagues will likely accept change at different rates. Some will immediately see the potential in your strategy. Others will take longer to come around. And some may interpret your strategy as abstract and not yet tangible. Resistance, passive or otherwise, should be expected from a minority of your constituents. Take the time to proactively communicate the direction you're taking your product, listen objectively to any concerns, and highlight the benefits for your organization. Remember, the energy you expend upfront will go a long way in enlisting the support you'll need to overcome any resistance to change down the road.

You'll find that some people are less comfortable thinking into the future and dealing with the inevitable changes. Change can be very threatening to people who are comfortable with the status quo. So be prepared to meet a degree of resistance as you meet with a broader group of your constituents. *Your goal is to align as many people as possible behind your strategy* and invite them to participate on the journey. The more that your extended team members understand where you'll be leading them, the more likely they are to support your activities and help you achieve your goals.

Take the time to patiently answer any questions that might arise. Pay particular attention to questions that challenge the direction you're taking. Think back to all the information you collected and internalized before developing your product strategy and the vetting you did with thought leaders, senior executives, and clients. You're well prepared to answer most questions. If you do get a question that you don't know the answer to, *don't bluff*. Get the answer and respond to the individual after the meeting.

Vesting the team members who will help you make your *shared* product strategy a reality is a critical step in the process. Product managers are ultimately accountable for getting results on behalf of the organization, but you cannot do it alone. You'll need the support of a wide variety of people across every function to enable your collective success. Laying out a compelling strategy and answering questions that arise with the facts you've accumulated will help you vest your organization and multiply the chances of your success.

CHAPTER FIVE'S TIPS FOR TAKING CHARGE

- To formulate a winning approach to the market, you must draw on all of the available information and use it to correctly anticipate shifts in your market *before* they happen. Your objective is to position your product to capitalize on the emerging opportunities you identify.

- To capitalize on market opportunities, the product strategy you create must be *directionally* correct. You're steering your product toward a point three to five years out. You'll be able to make incremental course corrections along the way.

- Capture your product strategy on a single slide that also details major milestones. Your organization, clients, and prospects will want to understand the journey you're taking them on. Framing the current, transitional, and future states allows you to tangibly discuss the path to achieving your product strategy.

- A strong product strategy needs to be tested on your senior executives, company thought leaders, customers, and prospects. By engaging with different parties and requesting that they challenge your strategy and underlying assumptions, you'll improve the end product and get them behind your plan.

- You'll likely need to develop a business case for any elements of your product strategy that extend beyond enhancing your existing product. Be prepared to outline the reasons your executive team should invest resources and what they can expect to see as a return on their investment.

- Vesting team members across the organization in your strategy will help make it a *shared* product strategy. This is a critical element of your future success and will multiply the odds in your favor. Product managers are ultimately accountable for getting desired results on behalf of the organization, but you cannot do it alone.

CHAPTER SIX: MOVING FROM VISION TO EXECUTION

My first shot sprang off the rim of the basket and bounced to the other end of the court. I had come to the gym to unwind and process the day's events. Thinking back, one meeting stood out from the rest: the one with Sinclair, Alex Wong, and Beth Swanson. It was only my second meeting with Beth, although it became apparent during the meeting that we would be working together closely. Beth had just accepted the lead project manager position and was also reporting directly to Sinclair. She was the person Sinclair counted on to handle thorny problems and identify potential issues *before* they blossomed into crises.

As I chased after the fleeing basketball, I played back the meeting. Sinclair had made it obvious that he'd be paying increased attention to the consistency of our company's execution. We were adding new team members weekly and new customers just as quickly. But as Beth had pointed out, our rapid growth was masking the fact that the hand-offs between product management, engineering, operations, customer service, and marketing were sloppy at best and non-existent at worst. It seemed that everyone was focusing on what they did best at the expense of having an effective process.

Sinclair had taken a balanced view of the situation and reminded the three of us that growing pains were to be expected. However, he was clearly concerned about the systemic hand-off issues and pointed out that the problems needed to be corrected quickly. Alex Wong, our head of engineering, had also been in the meeting and committed to working with Beth and me to improve our strained execution before things got out of hand.

I caught up to the wayward basketball and dribbled back up the court. Sinclair had asked Beth and me to put a product lifecycle framework in place that spelled out the *overall* process, including roles and deliverables. The process we implemented had to stretch from the inception of an idea to the retirement of any future product and effectively address the failed hand-offs between the different functions. Alex would partner with us in developing the framework.

Sinclair went on to say that while the product development framework that Alex and the product development team had been using during our start-up phase had worked well, he was not wedded to it. Sinclair and Alex would examine all the available options given our growth trajectory.

As I released a truer shot at the basket, I reflected on Sinclair's insights into our product development activities. He had observed that since stepping back from day-to-day involvement with the product, the engineering team had run with the ball and begun to drive the market requirements. Sinclair made it clear that he did not want the engineering team driving the requirements process and pointed out that *what we really needed were two processes:* an effective product development process — Waterfall, Agile, or a blended approach — and most importantly, *a market-focused process.*

Sinclair informed Beth and Alex that it was my role to own the market process, including requirements, and ultimately bridge both processes, just as he had done. Sinclair had also said that the product requirement gathering process he used needed to be modified because the company was no longer a start-up. He recognized that the interactive requirements-gathering process that Alpha Technology Ventures had used, with a small subset of early adopters, needed to evolve as the client base matured. The company was adding new customers rapidly, but it also had to satisfy the needs of its core revenue-generating customers. As the ball *swished* through the net, I hustled after it and mulled over his comments.

Before Sinclair recruited me into product management, he had been acting as the product manager and knew the details of the development team's processes. He understood that the company had reached the point where customers were expecting to see product roadmaps and that they were going to hold us accountable for delivering on our market promises.

Everyone in the meeting was aware that most of our current development activities missed on one or more legs of the three-legged stool of scope, schedule, and cost. This would need to be tightened up going forward. Today, only 48 percent of our product development projects actually met all three criteria. Beth had been keeping track, correctly anticipating that product development was going to become an area of increased focus.

The meeting had wrapped up with a 30-day deadline for Beth, Alex, and I to have a significantly improved process in place that enhanced our execution. Sinclair asked Beth to partner with me because she was much more conversant in technology terminology then I was. He knew I was going to need a translator.

As Beth, Alex, and I walked out of the meeting together, Sinclair offered one final piece of advice. He reminded us that our company's collective execution *"was only as strong as the weakest link in the chain."* As the day's stress melted away with each shot at the basket, I realized that I still had a lot to learn. I launched my next shot keenly aware that I was going to be spending a lot of evenings in the gym ...

PRODUCT LIFECYCLE MANAGEMENT FRAMEWORK

Sinclair has just helped Sean make the transition from product strategy to tactical execution. The first step of driving execution is to understand the expectations. Sinclair has made it very clear that he's expecting improved coordination between the various functions supporting the product lifecycle and that the company needs a new process that looks at product activities holistically. Sinclair has challenged Sean and Beth — within the next 30 days — to define the operational framework that will guide products from an idea to ultimate retirement.

He also expects Sean to improve the market-focused processes that support requirement gathering and prioritization because the existing start-up processes are no longer as effective as they once were. This resulted from the company's need to not only attract new clients *but also support a growing base of existing clients.*

As Sean and Beth just learned, the infrastructure currently in place has primarily focused on departmental responsibilities and seemingly neglects the transition points between the functions. This is not uncommon in companies at early stages of growth, but as a company moves into the domain of a mid-sized organization with an established customer base, this is a recipe for disaster.

Internal inefficiencies create the potential for significant customer-facing problems that can adversely affect your company's revenue stream. As you begin to take control of your product's development, you'll need to fully understand the PLM maturity of your organization to increase your effectiveness.

What is product lifecycle management? PLM is a methodology that clarifies and then integrates cross-functional product activities — information, people, and processes throughout the product lifecycle.

PLM is used to establish well understood cross-functional product practices, across rapidly growing and increasingly complex organizations, to increase efficiency and reduce execution risk.

WHERE DID PLM ORIGINATE?

The **PLM framework** was first adopted in the complex automotive and aerospace businesses and later spread to other industries. It is an outgrowth of the "lean" movement, which focuses on eliminating waste and inefficiencies from manufacturing processes.

The term **product lifecycle management** is often confused with the term **software development lifecycle** (SDLC). The software development lifecycle is a subcomponent of the PLM process. Although the overarching PLM process focuses on successfully managing a product through its various stages, the SDLC process is focused on increasing the efficiency, repeatability, and transparency of the software development process.

All companies have a set of organic business processes that enable a product to move through development to market. Start-up and mid-sized companies may use informal processes or follow a well-documented manual process. More mature companies with complex products automate the entire process across states, countries, partners, and various time zones.

Regardless of the size of your organization, having a PLM framework in place helps each participant in the product lifecycle understand the overall process, their role, and what is expected of them. It also allows the company to create standardized deliverables that other parties involved in the process are *counting on to do their jobs.*

PRODUCT LIFECYCLE

The term **product lifecycle** refers to a marketing concept which asserts that a product progresses through four separate stages during its life span: introduction, growth, maturity, and eventual decline.

Let's look more closely at the process framework that Sean, Alex, and Beth developed to strengthen their company's execution and meet Sinclair's request (Figure 6-1).

Your first observation is likely that the process Sean and Beth developed is linear. The process begins with the first stage, strategy, and ultimately ends with retirement.

There are seven phases in all:

- Strategy
- Requirements
- Analysis/Design
- Development
- Deployment
- Operation
- Retirement

Although the process is linear, notice that certain phases contain iterative cycles (depicted by arrows.) These iterative phases are strategy, requirements, analysis/design, and development. Each may require iteration or continued refinement before moving to the next step.

The next line shows activities associated with that stage. Note that there are 12 different activities that take place over the course of a product's life at Alpha Technology Ventures:

- Strategy (development)
- Business case (justification)
- Roadmap
- Requirements
- Plan
- Analysis
- Design
- Build
- Test
- Deploy
- Operate
- Retire

FIGURE 6-1. ALPHA TECHNOLOGY VENTURES' COMPLETED PRODUCT LIFECYCLE MANAGEMENT FRAMEWORK

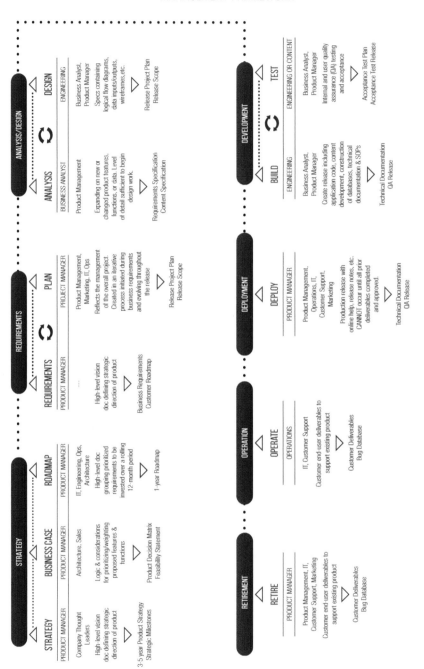

(Due to space constraints, Figure 6-1 is wrapped to two lines in this example. But if you were creating this in a spreadsheet, it would be a linear flow from left to right.)

The very first activity is strategy development, which we covered in an earlier chapter, and the final activity ends with a products retirement or discontinuation.

Take a close look at Figure 6-2, which isolates the first stage — strategy.

FIGURE 6-2. ALPHA TECHNOLOGY VENTURES' COMPLETED PRODUCT LIFECYCLE MANAGEMENT FRAMEWORK

STRATEGY		
STRATEGY	BUSINESS CASE	ROADMAP
PRODUCT MANAGER	PRODUCT MANAGER	PRODUCT MANAGER
Company Thought Leaders	Architecture, Sales	IT, Engineering, Ops, Architecture
High-level vision doc defining strategic direction of product	Logic & considerations for prioritizing/weighting proposed features & functions	High-level doc grouping prioritized requirements to be invested over a rolling 12-month period
3-5 year Product Strategy Strategic Milestones	Product Decision Matrix Feasibility Statement	1-year Roadmap

Note that the activity row indicates that first step in the process begins with strategy development, followed by business case and roadmap development. Underneath the activities, who ultimately owns the strategy development activity is listed, in this case the owner is you, the product manager. The fourth row outlines collaborators, the extended team members that help you complete the activity you own. As you can see, the collaborators in strategy development are your company's thought leaders. The fifth row contains a brief description of the deliverables that you're responsible for. After the final arrow, the formal names of the deliverables for each activity are listed: 3-5 year product strategy and strategic milestones.

WORD TO THE WISE!

Too often those at the end of the process, for example operations or customer service, are not included in relevant cross-functional meetings at earlier stages of the production process. This often leads to costly problems downstream when a product is being readied for market. Including extended team members early helps identify and prevent costly errors that could be avoided.

This same process would be followed through each of the seven phases and 12 activities of Alpha Technology Ventures' product lifecycle. Once complete it would look something like Figure 6–1.

As you can see, a completed product lifecycle management framework provides a comprehensive view of everyone involved in the lifecycle process. At Alpha Technology Ventures, the parties span various functions including product management, project management, architecture, engineering, operations, customer service, and marketing. By outlining the overall product production process, the hand-offs become very clear. Once everyone understands their roles, deliverables, and linkages, efficiency increases. An added benefit to having a standardized process is that it allows you to map out where you need cross-functional team meetings. This helps business owners ensure that particular product initiatives are on track, and quickly intervene if they are not.

IF YOU'RE STARTING A PLM FRAMEWORK FROM SCRATCH

Start by communicating the need for a standardized process that clarifies roles and responsibilities and reduces the chance that internal inefficiencies will adversely impact your company's revenue stream. Then solicit the support of your project management team. Project managers are tremendously helpful in pulling all the pieces together into a coherent process. Next, reach out to the head of engineering and see whether the engineering team has mapped out their production processes. Engineering is a great place to start because a large number of production activities take place within this functional area. Then collaborate with the other functional areas of your company to capture their processes. Once you have the baseline, work to identify gaps and make needed improvements to the existing processes.

Now that we have examined Alpha Technology Ventures' new PLM framework, it's time for you to investigate whether your company has created something similar. A documented PLM process is your map of your product's operational practices. What you learn about the maturity of your company's process, or lack thereof, will tell you what type of day-to-day challenges you need to be prepared to tackle.

The first step in your investigation should be to determine who owns the PLM process. Start with the project management team since, like product managers, they cross the functional boundaries of the organization. As we discussed earlier, the PLM framework cannot exist inside of functional boundaries. *It must cross functional boundaries* to ensure better alignment and reduce execution issues related to departmental hand-offs.

If there is no documented process in place, collaborate with other key participants to help define the PLM process for your organization.

COMMONLY CONFUSED TERMINOLOGY!

The term product lifecycle management is often confused with the term software development lifecycle (SDLC). The software development lifecycle is a subcomponent of the PLM process. Although the overarching PLM process focuses on successfully managing a product through its various stages, the SDLC process is focused on increasing the efficiency, repeatability, and transparency of the software development process.

PRODUCT DECISION-MAKING FRAMEWORK

Now that you have a thorough understanding of your company's product lifecycle management process, or lack thereof, we can turn our attention to your role in gathering market requirements and using them to create product roadmaps. Both of these activities reside firmly within your area of responsibility as a product manager.

Let's begin by discussing the process of requirements gathering. An important aspect of your job is to capture the inputs that form the foundation of the one-year rolling operational product plan known as a product roadmap. It is important to understand that *inputs are not requirements*. Inputs are individual elements of market information that need to be gathered and analyzed to determine whether a single input or multiple incidents of an input represent a market need.

Companies gather inputs in many different ways. Some organizations take an "inside out" approach. They primarily rely on internal experts or visionaries who possess a unique insight into the market, focus on their observations about clients' needs, and use these insights as the central inputs. Companies that follow this approach are often focused on creating disruptive products. Other organizations take a more conventional "outside in" approach by collecting inputs from clients, determining which are the most important, and feeding them into the product development process.

The first step in developing requirements is to determine which product management methodology you plan to use: voice of the customer, workflow, or outcomes. If you chose either of the first two options, it is useful to identify all the available sources of market inputs; this is step two.

As we discussed earlier, inputs exist throughout your organization. Your sales team collects inputs from their various dealings with customers. The customer service team captures inputs through their interactions with clients, online client communities, and the issue-resolution process. Your professional services team is an outstanding source of inputs since they spend significant amounts of time "living" at the client site. Consultants frequently incubate new ideas that can be turned into products. Research and development teams often identify new capabilities that can be productized. Products frequently have built-in feedback loops that allow you to collect client suggestions. Don't forget that you'll be in the field conducting research based upon whatever product management methodology you selected, producing additional inputs. All of these sources and others we did not discuss create a universe of inputs.

The third step in developing requirements is to collect relevant inputs into a central repository and convert the data into a useful form. There are several reasons why these inputs have never been centralized in most organizations. The first reason is that there was never a single person responsible for this activity. Second, collecting this data initially is laborious and requires good analytic skills to put it into a useable form. Third, inputs by themselves have little value unless there is a rational framework for interpreting them and turning them into something that can create value. So unless there is a tool in place to turn inputs into requirements, the effort would not be worth the time invested.

The next step is to create a rational framework for evaluating the centralized inputs and turning the inputs into prioritized requirements. Many organizations rely on judgments made by product managers, based on the depth of their market knowledge, to determine which capabilities should be invested in. But there are downsides to this approach. There are sure to be individuals that do not agree with your experience-based prioritization. Others may view your decisions as *subjective* and you may not have the facts to back up your beliefs. If you make a great call, you'll be heralded for your achievement. But if your product effort does not succeed, the ramifications can be equally significant. I refer to this model as "heroic" product management.

THE POWER OF OBJECTIVITY

Objective data, free from bias, is your most powerful ally. Everyone has opinions, but few people have the facts. When it comes to making decisions about your products, seek to gather as many facts as possible. This approach will proactively defuse problems and save time and energy that would be more effectively spent on creating value for your clients and company.

While heroic product management can work, it is often more productive to use an *objective* product decision-making framework called a product decision matrix. The general concept is that you'll create a tool with which to objectively evaluate the centralized inputs and turn them into a prioritized list of requirements for cross-functional vetting.

You begin by drafting the metrics you intend to use to filter the centralized inputs. When you have a draft in hand, you'll present it to your senior leadership team for buy-in. This will align your senior leadership behind the decisions you're going to make and reduce the chance that dissonant voices will disrupt the flow of your future prioritization efforts.

Once you and your colleagues agree on the metrics, you can talk with everyone in the PLM framework about how you'll be making prioritization decisions. Explaining the rationale behind your decisions will help your colleagues understand the process you're using and will likely increase support. You'll also find it useful when you need to tell clients why you chose to prioritize one set of requirements over another. The requirements that rise to the top of the product decision matrix will become the foundation of your product roadmap.

If you think about it, your company invests tremendous resources developing products. The PLM framework we just examined illustrates all the resources that are invested in identifying, building, sustaining, and retiring products. Virtually every part of the organization plays a part. Your company's product or service is the life blood of the company. The sales team identifies and contractually captures sources of revenue, but the products represent the value being sold. Given how important successful products are to your organization, shouldn't the major players agree on the logic that moves a product requirement to the top of the decision matrix?

By gaining upfront agreement to the business logic, you lift the veil of subjectivity that often creates organizational conflict and change the dynamic of the conversation.

FIGURE 6-3. ALPHA TECHNOLOGY VENTURE'S PRODUCT DECISION MATRIX FRAMEWORK

Categories and relative weight	Score	Source of the Input (33%)						Alignment with Strategy and Company Objectives (57%)						Aids Other Products (10%)	
		Number of Requests	Client	Sales	R&D	Customer Service	Product Management	Supports product vision	Market leadership	Regulatory compliance	Anticipated revenue	Margin	Estimated cost	Existing	New
Requirement	Score														
New indicators	98.5	18	5	8	1	3	1	x	x	n/a	moderate	high	low	x	
Dynamic drilling	96	10	5	3	1		1	x	x	n/a	moderate	high	low	x	
Executive dashboard	94	11	4	2	1	3	1	x	x	n/a	high	moderate	high		x
Mobile viewing	94	15	7	6		1	1	x	x	n/a	low	moderate	high	x	
Wireless capability	92	4		2	1		1	x	x	n/a	low	moderate	high	x	

Once the criteria for making prioritization decisions are agreed upon, the focus of the conversation shifts to execution.

Let's take a closer look at Figure 6-3, which outlines the three primary product decision filters (criteria) that Sean intends to propose to his senior leadership team:

- Source of the input
- Alignment with product strategy (vision) and company business objectives
- Ability to leverage product investment in multiple areas of the business

The first criterion that Sean has decided to use is the quality of the information. He has identified two components: primary information, defined as inputs *directly* conveyed to product management by customers, and secondary information that did not come directly from a customer. Sean has also decided that while the source is important, *frequency matters as well.* Requests that come in frequently should be given higher priority than those that are captured only once.

His second criterion reflects company and product business objectives. Sean has decided that there are six key subcomponents within this section:

- Alignment with his product strategy
- Market leadership
- Regulatory compliance
- Anticipated revenue
- Margin
- Cost

Notice that the first two subcomponents, alignment with product strategy and market leadership, are specific to his product. Sean is indicating that identified product opportunities that help him attain his product strategy should be prioritized higher than requests that do not align with the overall product strategy. He also wants to invest in those ideas that help him achieve his objective of becoming *the* market leader.

The third subcomponent tackles the need to handle regulatory compliance issues as they arise. Alpha Technology Ventures serves a market that is subject to governmental regulation. Sean and the senior leadership cannot afford to ignore new regulations. To eliminate the legal risk of not complying with new regulations, any new regulatory requirements will need to be addressed as a matter of high importance.

The last three subcomponents relate to maintaining the financial health of the organization and the product. Sean is suggesting that the inputs that have the most significant revenue potential need to be prioritized highest. He is also following a similar logic with margin. However, Sean recognizes that the relative cost of development also needs to be considered, since high revenue and a high cost of development might diminish the potential returns.

The third criterion that Sean is proposing is investment. Sean believes that if an investment in his product can also benefit other products, it should generate a higher rating than if the investment can only benefit one product.

Sean has gone one step further in refining his decision-making criteria. Because the benefits of these sections differ, he has decided to weight each one. Sean decided to allocate 33 percent to the source of the input category. He gave the business metrics section 57 percent, and the ability to leverage an investment over multiple areas 10 percent.

Within each section, every subcomponent has its own weighting. For example, client requests are 12 percent of the total. These individual weightings roll up to the section weightings.

Sean's product decision matrix clearly lays out the logic he is using to make decisions. The metrics you use will depend on your business needs. The product decision matrix is a handy tool with which to analyze the centralized inputs and calculate which inputs should mathematically rise to the top, given your criteria.

Take a closer look at the product decision matrix framework that Sean just created in Figure 6–3.

After he scored the inputs, Sean decided to take one more step — to form a cross-functional team to evaluate the top 20 items for potential inclusion in his first product roadmap.

LEVERAGING CROSS-FUNCTIONAL TEAMS AT THIS PHASE

If you've followed the same path as Sean and created your own product decision matrix, you now have a prioritized list of high-level requirements. These requirements list, in descending importance, opportunities your organization has to create value for customers and your organization. You're probably eager to plot out where these requirements go on your product roadmap. Before you do that, it's useful to form a standing cross-functional team of members from the various functional areas of your business who support your product. There are very important reasons for doing this.

By assembling a team to review the list of prioritized requirements, you're able to *look at each requirement from an operational perspective and identify potential issues before they happen.* For example, you might find an item at the top of your list has a high score, but the technology does not yet exist to capitalize on this market opportunity.

Or perhaps there isn't sufficient customer service or professional service resources in place to support a prioritized requirement. These types of issues will affect your roadmap planning and can only be discovered by assembling knowledgeable people from the various functions. It is critically important that you use the 360 degree perspective of your cross-functional team to catch potential execution issues before you start to invest dollars in a requirement that you'll not be able to bring to market!

Another reason to form a cross-functional team is to increase buy-in. If your colleagues are involved in the decision-making process, they'll be more likely to support the direction you're taking.

You'll need to lead and facilitate the meeting. Given how much time you've spent developing the priorities, you might feel particularly invested in a certain outcome. That's only natural. But you need to remain objective. Assessing these highly ranked requirements should be a dynamic process — you need to encourage open dialogue about every topic and its relative placement on the prioritization list. The team that you've assembled is there to help you fill in any blind spots. By encouraging an open discussion, you'll increase buy-in from your colleagues and help align your team.

Keep in mind that you've not yet defined the scope of the requirement because you're not yet sure if an item is going to make the final cut. We will talk about this in an upcoming chapter.

Your cross-functional team will also begin communicating your final product prioritization decisions, whether you want them to or not. There is tremendous value in empowering your team members to communicate the team's decisions to their functional counterparts on your behalf. There is often a tribal element to human organizations, and the functional members of your team can help channel important information back to their counterparts on your behalf. Peer-to-peer communication can be quite powerful. Just make sure that you establish some ground rules concerning what gets communicated and that the group is in agreement about the priorities.

If you're now convinced of the value in forming a cross-functional team, let's talk about how you go about doing so. There are several things you'll want to consider.

The first is selecting the right people. You should strive to incorporate individuals who are knowledgeable about your product, good team contributors, and influential with their counterparts. Although it is generally positive to have a team that comes to consensus easily, be careful not to stack the deck with people who will agree to your prioritization without challenging your logic. It's best to have a range of divergent perspectives so you can see all the available options and make a better decision. This means that you may want to add several people to the team who hold divergent views from your own — as long as they can work effectively within the team dynamic! Seeking out different perspectives generally leads to a better outcome as long as the fabric of the team is not shredded.

You'll also want to consider geographic location. It is preferable to have your cross-functional team members in one room when reviewing the prioritized list of requirements. There are several reasons for this. It can be difficult for remote team members to stay actively engaged in half-day meetings reviewing your list of requirements. Additionally, you'll have a more difficult time gauging a remote team member's degree of buy-in if you're unable to assess their body language. Given the nature of business today, with geographically distributed teams being common, gathering team members in one location is not always possible. But if you're choosing between two equally qualified candidates and one is centrally located, consider adding the local individual as opposed to the one that is more geographically remote.

With these points in mind, begin drawing up your list of possible candidates. Make sure to list two people from each functional area in case your preferred candidate is not available or interested in joining your team. Once you have the list in hand, reach out to the functional leader of each area. Explain the purpose of your cross-functional team and the fact that you're looking to add representatives from each department to provide input into the prioritization process. Tell them you would like to add your preferred candidate to the team and explain the amount of time you expect to require for these meetings. Depending on your organization, this can range from once a year to once a quarter. Then ask for their support.

After you've met with each functional leader and gained their support, contact potential team members and explain that you met with their boss and requested their time. Explain the mission of the group and what you're looking for (i.e., their active participation, candid feedback, outbound communication, and support). Most people are excited to have a voice in shaping the direction of their company's product and will jump at the chance to join your team. Make sure that you've selected the date of your first meeting when you talk to your new team member so they know when you'll meet for the first time.

You're now ready to hold your first meeting. Be sure to start by reviewing the mission and answering any questions. Explain the frequency you expect the group to meet. Then distribute the top 20 prioritized items and begin working your way through them. Explore each item in detail and determine its feasibility. This will generally take half a day. Once you've worked through the list, explain your expectations regarding outbound communication and make sure that the group is aligned behind the priorities.

Congratulations! You're now ready to create your product roadmap.

DEVELOPING PRODUCT ROADMAPS

With a prioritized list of requirements in hand that has been vetted by your cross-functional counterparts for operational feasibility, you're ready to begin developing a draft product roadmap. A product roadmap is an operational plan that highlights your products quarterly development activity over a *rolling* 12 months. Each planned deliverable, otherwise known as a release, is thoughtfully slotted into a calendar quarter over the course of your annual plan. Items placed on the roadmap provide a high-level description of each release and are not intended to communicate detailed scope or cost information.

Product releases generally fall into one of three categories: new value creation, maintenance and support of an existing product, or investment in an internal capability that is not visible to your clients, but necessary to produce your product.

- **A new value creation release** is a new product, component, capability, or feature that provides customers with increased value. These types of releases are the centerpiece of your development efforts and are intended to grow the revenue stream of your company.

- **Maintenance and support releases** are updates to existing customer-facing products that preserve the product's revenue stream. This type of investment does not create new value but it does enable customers to continue to extract the expected value from your product.

- **Internal product releases** are investments made in the components of your offering *that are not seen by customers.* Internal products help support the day-to-day operations of your offering and are required to enable your product to generate value for your customers. These investments are often neglected during roadmap planning because they are out of sight and therefore easier to put off or ignore.

All three of these categories are necessary to keep your product healthy and valuable in the eyes of your revenue-generating customers. Regardless of your company's size, there are only so many development resources available. It can be tricky to work out the right mix of releases to maximize your market effectiveness. *Your job as a product manager is to balance these three types of releases to fuel or sustain market growth.*

Now that we have discussed the different types of releases, let's turn our focus to the roadmap itself and the intended audiences. Most organizations have *one roadmap per product or family of related products.* This roadmap is used for a variety of internal and external communication purposes as well as expectations management.

DECLINE IN THE OUTPUT OF YOUR VALUE CREATION ACTIVITIES

Companies often underestimate the resources required to sustain an existing product after its initial release. As products mature, they tend to consume a greater percentage of your available development resources. The more FTEs consumed supporting existing products, the fewer resources that are available for new value creation activities. Over time, the number of customer-facing product releases can decline as more resources are consumed supporting existing products.

Internally, roadmaps are used to *coordinate cross-functional activities* in support of a release. Whether they indicate development team activity or sales and marketing readiness, the release dates on your roadmap signal when internal efforts must be complete to ensure a smooth transition from product development to market introduction. A variety of internal activities need to take place for this to happen. Your company's internal staff must be trained on the new products' capabilities to support client inquiries, marketing must be prepared to get the message out, and sales must be made ready to communicate the value of the release to clients. In essence, the release date on a roadmap serves to trigger a series of required activities that ensures everyone inside your organization is ready to support the market release and maximize the revenue opportunity.

Product roadmaps are also used to *manage the expectations of internal constituents.* Your well thought-out roadmap acts at the cornerstone of your operational activities. It firmly communicates the direction you're taking your product in support of your product strategy. Colleagues from across your organization will know what to expect and what not to expect over the next 12 months.

ALWAYS PREPARE INTERNAL TEAM MEMBERS IN ADVANCE

Make it your policy to alert client-facing colleagues to the substance of an outbound message before communicating directly with clients. This does not mean that you need to ask for their permission, but you should strive to ensure that your counterparts are never shocked or surprised by any of your customer communications. Adopting this approach shows respect for your colleagues and the relationships they have developed with clients. It's important that your colleagues are never put in an awkward position and perceived as being out of the loop, which can damage their credibility.

Product roadmaps also act as a means for senior leadership to *keep track of your product development team's productivity.* Your company has made significant investments in people, technology, and processes and the senior leadership team will want to get the results they expect. Product roadmaps are one of the ways they can keep track of your team's success or failure.

From an external perspective, product roadmaps are used to *help manage client expectations.* As your customer base increases, so does the volume of inputs. The customers who use your products will expect you to continually invest in your offering and increase its value over time. Roadmaps are used to help manage existing client expectations by communicating to the various parties what you're planning to invest in.

Roadmaps are also used as *part of the sales process.* Product managers often go into the field to support key sales activities and discuss both the direction of the product and the tactical activities planned for the coming year. Sales teams excel at selling the capabilities of a product as it exists today, but no one is more knowledgeable about where the product is headed than you!

TIME TO ESTABLISH ANOTHER POLICY!

Once you've developed your roadmap, you'll need to establish a policy on how much product roadmap information you want to share with customer-facing colleagues and clients.

You might be willing to share more in a less competitive market than in a highly competitive one. The key is to balance the need for communication against the risk that competitors might beat you in developing a capability that would give you a market advantage. Your policy needs to help you balance the risks and rewards.

PRODUCT ROADMAPS ARE CENTRAL TO EFFECTIVELY MANAGING EXPECTATIONS

As you can see, roadmaps are used for a variety of internal and external purposes. Product roadmaps are used internally to coordinate cross-functional support, manage employee expectations, drive accountability, and measure team productivity. Contrast this with the external expectations of managing client expectations and supporting the sales process with key clients. Although you can try to use one document to address all these needs, it's not a perfect solution. It's often more effective to create two types of product roadmaps: internal and external.

To successfully address these wide-ranging internal and external expectations, product roadmaps need to be broken into two separate documents with linked information. You will use the external roadmap to build trust with clients and support the sales process. The internal roadmap's goals are more aggressive — to support value creation and accountability.

The internal roadmap will be used by you, the product manager, the product development team, and your senior leadership *for performance improvement*. This roadmap will never leave the building and never be seen by clients. You'll use it to measure the product team's success at meeting all three legs of the stool: scope, cost, and schedule. For accountability purposes, if you miss one of the three legs, the release was not a success.

There is often a raging debate about which is more important: schedule or scope. This implies that successful scope and schedule cannot coexist. Nothing could be further from the truth. Creating an internal roadmap will allow you to establish a baseline and work to improve the components (people, process, and tools) until your company consistently executes on all three. By holding the internal team to a higher standard than what you show the market, your execution should improve over time, but not at the cost of undermining client trust.

The customer-facing teams will use the information contained in the external roadmap to manage client expectations and support sales activity. So that you don't promise more than you can deliver, this document should be less aggressive than the internal roadmap. However, it should show the releases that you're convinced you can achieve within the specified timeframes. As company execution improves, you can add more items to your external roadmap. Frequently missing your market commitments undermines trust and over time will damage your company's client relationships and reputation. Customers will trust your organization when you demonstrate that "you do what you say" and execute your roadmap consistently.

By splitting your draft roadmap into two pieces — one to address internal needs and one to manage client expectations and support the sales process, you can optimize execution and build trust with your client base simultaneously.

CHAPTER SIX'S TIPS FOR TAKING CHARGE

- As you make the transition from creating a strategy for your product to taking a leadership role in execution, start by determining whether your company has developed a product lifecycle management process. A documented PLM process is your map to the operational practices of your product. What you learn about the maturity of your company's process, or lack thereof, will tell you what type of day-to-day challenges you need to be prepared to tackle.

- The PLM process outlines your company's product production processes, but it does not enable you to turn the inputs that your company collects into meaningful market requirements that will generate value for your customers. A product decision matrix enables you to transform inputs into requirements and gain organizational agreement to the objective metrics you'll use to make investment decisions going forward.

- Once you've filtered your inputs through the product decision matrix and generated your initial list of prioritized requirements, form a standing cross-functional team and examine each requirement from an operational perspective. This will help you identify potential market execution issues *before* you invest in product development activity and increase the level of buy-in from your colleagues.

- Use a product roadmap to illustrate the product development activity you plan to take over a rolling 12 months. Your roadmap will also address a wide range of internal and external expectations, from communication to accountability. Rather than relying on a single product roadmap to cover all these needs, break your roadmap into two separate documents: an external roadmap, which you'll use to support the sales process and build trust with the client base, and an internal roadmap for accountability.

CHAPTER SEVEN: PRODUCT DEVELOPMENT

The candy bars on Alex's desk were vanishing quickly. I had just walked over to his office to talk to him about our need to collaborate more. As I settled into a chair, two of his engineering confidants were helping themselves to the chocolates. Seeing the reasonably serious look on my face, they had decided to load up before heading back to their cubicles.

As they left, I thought about how much easier it was to work with the engineering team. I had learned an incredible amount over the last six months. Beth had been particularly helpful — she answered any of my technology-related questions as the need arose, which had been often. Sinclair was right: I needed a technology translator. Beth understood the business needs and the technology lingo; without her support the learning curve would have been much steeper.

While my comfort level had increased, we still had a long way to go. In fact, taking our collaboration to the next level is what brought me to Alex's communal candy bowl. As head of engineering, Alex played a critical role in our products' success. Sinclair had recently mentioned that our collective product development execution was not improving as quickly as it should, and I thought I knew why. As Alex's team members left the room, I opened the conversation.

"Alex, thanks for making time for me. Hopefully I didn't interrupt anything important?" I asked, just to make sure I had not interrupted a serious meeting rather than an informal chat. Alex shook his head, reached for one of the surviving chocolates and said, "no, they were here to talk about a problem we encountered during our most recent builds. It looks like they have a solution that's going to work, and they want me to look at the code." Alex looked confident, which was always a good sign when it came to my product. "What brings you over here, Sean?" Alex inquired while tossing his wrapper into a nearly overflowing trash can.

Before answering the question, I walked over to Alex's door and closed it and then reached for a candy bar myself. As I sat back down and opened the wrapper, I candidly said, "Alex, I was hoping we could talk about how to improve our alignment. Sinclair let me know he doesn't think we're clicking on all cylinders. I'm sure you've had a similar conversation with him," I let my voice trail off, seeking confirmation. Alex paused before responding, "Sinclair and I have had several conversations along those lines. He's pushing me to pick up the pace and consistency of our product development execution. He indicated that if we can't meet the new performance criteria, he'll have me look at offshoring aspects of our development to get a better result. Between you and me, Sean, I would prefer not to have to do that." Alex looked genuinely pained at the thought.

"Well, now that I know we're on the same page, I think this conversation will be easier," I thought to myself, reassured that I was not overstepping. "I've been giving this some serious thought and I think you and I need to see if we can come up with some creative ideas to further improve our alignment. I spoke with Beth about a couple of ideas that I've been kicking around and she says, as long as you agree, we should implement them." Alex looked interested, since anything that prevented sending engineering activities overseas would be welcome.

"So, what are your ideas, Sean?" Alex asked, genuinely interested. "I think most of our issues are related to not having aligned incentives," I stated simply. "Although we put a consistent PLM process in place, we didn't take the additional step of aligning our incentives. I think we need to change that." Alex looked open to the suggestion. "Also, I don't think our meeting structure is right. We need to do more to stay in sync and be sure we use our time and resources efficiently. I asked Beth to give some thought to creating a better meeting rhythm so your team doesn't end up having to do throwaway development like we've done in the past," I continued. Alex nodded his head in agreement.

"What do you think?" I asked. Alex looked thoughtful. After sitting back in his chair and staring out his window for a couple of seconds, he turned back my way and said, "Sean, I think your suggestions make sense. I have only one concern and that has to do with aligning incentives. To be frank, I feel pretty confident I can hit my objectives. So before I would sign up for aligned incentives I would want to understand what they are."

Attempting to reassure Alex, I said, "I understand where you're coming from, Alex, and I don't think all your objectives would need to change, but the tighter we can align your team's efforts with our market goals the more likely we are to achieve our company objectives. I'm convinced that we're not all pulling in the same direction. Assuming this works and we tighten our alignment and improve our execution, you might not need to investigate offshore firms. But if we keep going the way we are I don't think Sinclair will let up on looking at other options," I said.

With a considered stare, Alex decided to take the plunge, "Alright, I'm on board. What do you suggest as next steps?" Aware that what we had just agreed to was in everyone's best interest, I responded, "Why don't we call Beth and see if we can draft a proposal on your white board? Once we have something we think will work, we can jointly present it to Sinclair. With the three of us agreeing on what we need to do to continue to improve our market execution, Sinclair will likely support our proposal." As Alex once again nodded in agreement, I realized *we had come one step closer to being a truly aligned team with a common set of objectives.* As Alex picked up his phone to see if he could catch Beth, I picked up a marker and walked over to his white board.

As I started to sketch out several proposed objectives, I made a mental note to fill that bowl of chocolates the next time I was in Alex's office.

STAYING IN SYNC WITH THE DEVELOPMENT TEAM

Sean is a quick study. Over the last six months he has relied on Beth's knowledge of the development process to come up the learning curve quicker than he might have otherwise. His increased comfort working with the development team has helped him realize that more steps need to be taken to ensure strong alignment between the principles: project management, product management, and engineering. Sean clearly realizes that the PLM process Sinclair asked them to put into place clarified roles and responsibilities — but it did not resolve *all* of the alignment and accountability issues. Having come out of sales, Sean understands that incentives can be a powerful motivator and that the lack of aligned objectives currently has everyone rowing in different directions.

Aligning incentives focuses behavior and is likely to increase performance. The fact that Beth, Alex, and Sean are now drafting shared objectives to take to Sinclair demonstrates that they understand their importance. With project management, product management, and engineering all sharing a common set of performance-based objectives, Sinclair is more likely to get the performance he is demanding. When incentives are not aligned, each group is likely to work to meet their own goals, but they are not likely to achieve the optimal results that they could if they had shared aligned goals *as a team*.

Let's take a look at what they came up with. The new concept that they will present to Sinclair will be that the product manager, project manager, and engineers will become a unified team. They will all share responsibility for driving product development activity and a common set of goals and incentives. This newly unified team will benefit if the common goals are reached. Conversely, they will not reach their incentive payout if they miss these goals. The four goals will be:

- Achieving the company's projected sales and margin rates
- Publishing *fully resourced* product roadmaps
- Achieving 80 percent of customer-facing roadmap deliverables (defined as on time, on scope, and on budget)
- 100 percent compliance with the product lifecycle management process that was recently implemented

Now let's look at the logic behind each item. The team has decided that they will share the goal of achieving projected sales and margin rates. This goal makes the most sense for product management because Sean is accountable for identifying market opportunities that can be turned into revenue. He is also responsible for readying the customer-facing functions of the organization to support the sales process and for going into the field to support key sales activities. The project and engineering teams have also decided to share this goal even though their impact is less direct. Beth has agreed to it because her team is responsible for keeping releases on track. She believes that as long as Sean has selected the right elements to invest in, the company should generate the revenue it needs to attain its sales plan. Engineering has agreed because their efforts enable attainment of the sales and margin numbers, and because Alex believes it will make his team more responsive to client needs. Sinclair is likely to support this goal because it will align the value-creation team behind his goal of scaling the company.

AVOID QUICKSAND: WORK TOGETHER TO DEFINE ACCEPTABLE SCOPE

Many organizations are confused by this area. The hand-offs from product management to engineering — in terms of the specificity that will allow the engineering team to effectively estimate the amount of resources and give them enough clarity to begin development — are rarely smooth. It requires the teams to agree on documentation standards that work for everyone. Project management often needs to help define this standard and facilitate the overall process. This is particularly true when it comes to starting the development effort. Commonly, the development team will want all the details before initiating a project. But this is generally a mistake; there is no reason the project can't start sooner on the non-negotiable aspects of scope. Remember, the sooner value can be created for your customers and your organization, the better!

The second goal they'll propose is making sure the items that make the product roadmaps are fully resourced. This will require a significant amount of upfront collaboration and planning between product management, engineering, and project management. In the future, before any item is placed on the roadmaps, the engineering team, along with project management, will need to accurately estimate the time and resources needed to create a given requirement. Product management must communicate clearly about the scope of what is to be accomplished. Once the resource estimate is known, product management will need to make good decisions on the priorities. To successfully manage any future tradeoff conversations, Sean must be clear about how the priorities relate back to the business value the team is attempting to create.

The third goal is to achieve successful execution on roadmap deliverables. If you recall, only 48 percent of Alpha Technology Ventures' releases were on time, on scope, and on budget. Sinclair was not pleased with this level of performance and has been pressing the core team to improve. Alex, Beth, and Sean decided to put a stake in the ground that anything less than 80 percent was unacceptable. The team believes that by making improved execution a goal linked to compensation, they can significantly improve performance. Sinclair will no doubt be very pleased with this suggestion.

The final goal relates to adherence with the new PLM process. Beth, Alex, and Sean realize that having everyone adhere to the new process is important to continually improving their execution.

The team intends to ask Sinclair to replace four of their existing goals with these new ones. They believe that shared goals will significantly improve their execution and outcomes. With everyone pulling in the same direction and with bonus dollars at stake, Alex, Beth, and Sean believe this gives them the best chance to improve their product development execution.

The team has also decided to take an additional step: revising their cross-functional meeting structure. Beth has decided to hold a new series of coordinated meetings at standard intervals in the PLM process. The meetings will include the business owner and the internal cross-functional team members involved in product development. The objective is to make sure there is a business owner review with the extended team to agree to the plan, mitigate risks, and improve overall coordination. She has specified that the meetings will be held at the end of four PLM phases: Strategy, Requirements, Analysis/Design, and Development.

At the meeting at the end of the strategy phase, product management will facilitate the meeting and present the proposed new product capabilities to the internal cross-functional product development team. The goal is to answer the question, "Have we adequately defined the solution to capitalize on the market opportunities?" After this meeting addresses any questions and concerns, the team will move into the requirements phase of the PLM process.

WHAT IS A PROJECT PLAN?

A project plan is a document created by a project manager to model an approved project and guide its execution. It is the design document for *how* the project needs to be executed. Project managers deal with change. If all projects followed their original plans exactly, organizations wouldn't need project managers! The project plan enables the team to effectively communicate and proactively manage both change and expectations along the way. The plan contains information documenting the project's goals, scope, milestones, activities, resources, limitations, assumptions, and risks. Once a project is underway, the project plan and associated project schedule are compared with the actual project to effectively control the project and proactively report status and risks. Project plans are invaluable to successful product teams and help ensure effective communication between all the key stakeholders.

The second meeting would take place at the end of the requirements phase. Because this phase involves translating market requirements into functional specifications, the objective of this meeting is to establish a final set of expectations that clearly demonstrate that the commercial success criteria can be met. The content of this meeting would be presented by project management, product management, and the lead engineer, and would cover the system requirements and scope and gain agreement to the project plan. Assuming everyone was on board with the final requirements, scope, and project plan the team would move onto the design phase.

The third meeting would focus on the proposed design of the product or capability and seek approval from the business owner and buy-in from the extended cross-functional team members who would support the product post-development. Product management and the lead engineer would present the information. It is also when the team needs to ask, "What programs, plans, training, or other events are required to ensure a successful launch?"

The fourth and final meeting would be at the end of the development phase and represent the final go/no-go junction before the product would move into market deployment. This is the point where you need to be sure that your product is ready to launch, that all testing and refinement are complete, and that you've established the momentum needed to start selling. The cross-functional development team and the business owner would sign off before release.

Alex, Beth, and Sean have concluded that involving PLM process stakeholders and the business owner at critical junctures *throughout the entire development process* will increase efficiency. With improved coordination, aligned goals, and incentives, the team believes they can take the next step and significantly improve their execution.

You'll need to work with your counterparts inside your own organization to construct the optimal framework for your company. If possible, link the goals of your product team's principles with your own, in meaningful ways, and look to align incentives. Also, work closely with your project management team to ensure appropriate synchronization all the way through the development process, and develop a meeting rhythm that works for your business. Don't forget to gain agreement to the key deliverables in estimating projects and agree to a standard detailed scope document that enables your engineering team to take the next step.

> ## DIFFERENT NAMES FOR SOLVING A COMMON NEED
> When it comes to capturing requirements, the names used to describe the essential documents vary but the need remains the same. Some companies develop business requirements documents (BRDs), others focus on market requirements documents (MRDs) and product requirements documents (PRDs), or any combination of the three. To add to the confusion, the information in the documents is often interchangeable. The key to developing good requirements documents is to gain agreement on what information and what type of documentation is essential for your development team to turn your market requirements into reality.

FURTHER DEFINING REQUIREMENTS

The format for detailed requirements varies by business and often goes by different names. Regardless of what you call it, it is likely that many different people will contribute content to your requirements documentation. Given that requirements are so variable, let's discuss them at the outline level. The sections that Sean, Beth, and Alex agreed to are:

- About this document
- Business analysis
- High-level use cases
- Functional requirements
- Compliance requirements
- Report requirements
- User interface requirements
- Environment requirements

About this document — The first section frames several important points. The first is the history of the document; in other words, the date of the latest version, the version number, who made the most recent change, and a description of the revision. The document history is important because many people will contribute to the document and there will be numerous revisions. These specifics will outline who approved the document changes, usually the lead engineer, and the date approval took place. It is common to include a description of key terms as well to ensure that everyone involved is speaking the same language.

Business analysis and business requirements— The second section normally begins by describing the business need at a high level and then highlights the key business questions the new capability is attempting to address. This segment should also include a proposed release date tied to your product roadmap. It would then list any number of high-level business/market requirements, with associated descriptions, to be included in the release. If necessary, insert a SWOT analysis (a method used to evaluate strengths, weaknesses, opportunities, and threats) and any underlying assumptions related to the commercial value of the release. The final component of this section is a feature matrix.

FEATURE MATRIX

Feature matrixes are used to capture product development estimates for a prioritized list of features. The goal of this matrix is to provide a "cut off" line for product development based upon the available time, resources, and money. This quick estimating takes place before detailed technical analysis. Feature matrixes allow the team to make sure the scope of the envisioned project does not exceed the available resources.

High-level use cases — Use cases capture detailed business requirements, which are then turned into functional specifications for your product. This section often incorporates a diagram illustrating the system that the user is interacting with to receive value from the new capabilities you're developing. It might also list an actor hierarchy, if more than one party is using your product, and lists all the use cases that have been developed.

Functional requirements — These generally roll up into a use case; in other words, into the behavioral elements of how the product will be used. Functional requirements are the specific elements that define what a product is supposed to accomplish and are used to guide the design of the product.

Compliance requirements — Regulatory compliance refers to any rules, regulations, and requirements that are relevant to the product to meet a governing body's laws or mandated procedures. They might include data use rules, security, or contractual requirements or perhaps governmental obligations.

WHAT ARE REGULATORY AGENCIES?

Regulatory agencies are essentially independent government bodies that have been established by an act of law to set standards and enforce their use. Established standards have the force of law. You must adhere to them to avoid penalties.

Report requirements — The data would need to include inputs, layout, report fields, headers and footers, and any groupings.

User interface requirements — It might begin with a conceptual site map and detail the associated navigation. This information is often presented in a diagram detailing the analysis that has been conducted. If a protosite has been created to tangibly model the user interface capabilities, a hyperlink is often inserted for easy access.

Environment requirements — The final section outlines environment requirements. This would include architecture standards relating to system performance and any environment considerations as well as operational and integration requirements. In the case of Alpha Technology Ventures, environmental considerations might include browser platforms, system availability, disaster recovery, and response time.

Requirements documentation is "where the rubber meets the road." It is the point in the process where your high-level observations regarding market opportunities get translated into tangible capabilities by your engineering team. Establishing a mutually agreeable framework with sufficient detail to turn your observations into reality will be essential for your success.

LITMUS TEST

The goal of the product development phase is to document the function, performance, design constraints, and attributes of your new capabilities. The team's documentation must be complete, clear, unambiguous, and testable. If your business is similar to Alpha Technology Ventures, common deliverables during this phase might include prototypes, protosites, or protowikis. To ensure completeness and that all success criteria have been met, your team's detailed requirements must ultimately trace back to the prioritized market requirements that you established earlier.

MAINTAINING FLEXIBILITY

A tremendous amount of work goes into developing your priorities, roadmaps, and requirements. Given the work effort, it's easy to get locked into your plan and ignore developments in your marketplace that impact your activities. However, you need to set the stage for rapid changes to your plans *early* in your tenure as a product manager. Although you won't need to make rapid shifts in your strategy and tactics often, it is sure to happen.

One of the best things you can do, from the beginning, is to simply insert a footer on the bottom of your product decision matrix and product roadmaps indicating that your plans are subject to change based on market conditions. This should not be used to avoid accountability for performance, but to explain that you will need to make course corrections as market circumstances dictate. Making it clear, from the beginning, that you reserve the right to do so makes great sense. It helps if you do this before you ever need to draw on that card. If you wait until you have to make a change to alert people, you're likely to meet more resistance. As we discussed earlier, markets move, competitors develop new capabilities, acquisitions or mergers happen, and none of these are within the span of your control. A simple disclaimer can help you proactively manage through change when it occurs.

ITERATING WITH CUSTOMERS

Throughout the processes of identifying sources of information, developing a product strategy, creating your roadmaps, defining requirements, and ultimately designing your product, opportunities to interact with customers abound. You need to take advantage of these opportunities and interact as much as possible to refine your plans and improve your product offerings. While doing so, *remember to stay focused on detecting patterns and don't get caught up in individual observations.*

Most companies place a premium on refining their products with direct customer involvement, believing the more customers are involved in development, the more likely your company is to design products that meet client needs. In fact, many product development methodologies continue to migrate in the direction of minimizing documentation and reinvesting the time in iterative customer product development in the belief that more value is created.

It is hard to argue with this logic. Many tomes of detailed product documentation, representing hours and hours of work, are sitting on shelves collecting dust and we can easily question what value they created. Whether you're in product management, project management, or engineering the labor cost you represent is not insignificant and companies want to get the maximum return on their investment in you. This observation has not been lost on all the people involved in creating valuable products and services. In fact, these observations have led to an increased focus on customer engagement at all stages of the product development cycle.

The key to maximizing your engagement opportunities is to have a well-defined plan and objective. Taking a structured approach lets customers know that you value their time and that you're serious about listening to what they have to say. Each time you engage with clients, they are assessing you and your organization. So it is important to have a well-thought-out plan.

Start by defining an objective. What are you hoping to accomplish? Do you want candid feedback on your product strategy or roadmap? Are you looking to walk customers through a new prototype of your product and solicit input? Perhaps you want to investigate different pricing scenarios and identify the best option? Or are you investigating your client's workflow processes?

Depending on what you want to accomplish, your next step is to choose the forum that works best. There are several different types of engagement opportunities:

- Site visits
- Surveys
- Virtual meetings
- Visits to your corporate location
- Regional client meetings
- Client conferences
- Focus groups

WHAT ARE FOCUS GROUPS?

A focus group is a research setting where a small number of relatively similar individuals are selectively invited to disclose personal perceptions and behaviors regarding your product or strategy. An experienced moderator guides participants through the discussion, encouraging divergent view-points. Focus groups are usually not one-time events; they are often repeated in a number of locations to get a broad view of the topic being investigated.

It often helps to have tools or visual aids. Client conversations are much easier if you provide a framework for the discussion. Walk them through your product strategy, reveal your roadmap quarter by quarter, demonstrate your prototype, or have a framework that explains your different pricing scenarios. Going in blind and asking questions will not reflect well on you or your organization. Take the time to develop a useful visual aid before beginning the dialog. Prepare structured questions that help pinpoint the value you're attempting to extract from the meeting and don't be afraid to continually refine your questions as you go along. It is highly probable that as you learn more from your interactions with clients, you'll want to revise some of your original assumptions. That's why you're engaging with clients in the first place, to improve your product. Be flexible and make the necessary adjustments as you come up the learning curve. Be sensitive to your client's time. Ask upfront how much time is available and stick to the timeline unless the client voluntarily extends it. Also explain how you intend to use the information they have shared and what your next steps are.

Over the years, I've learned it's very beneficial to send a note thanking clients for their time. It builds good will and shows that you value their time and input and you're willing to make an effort to acknowledge that. Regardless of the medium you choose, it's useful in further developing your company's relationship with a client.

ADVISORY COUNCILS ARE YOUR BOARD OF DIRECTORS!

There is an inherent danger in staffing your advisory council with important customers that can dictate the course of your products in a direction that won't benefit the *majority* of your customers. Remember, your advisory council was created to thoughtfully advise you on key decisions and help you look at things from your most insightful customers' perspective. They are your board of directors, and when boards begin to tell CEOs how to run their business they are often on the ropes. Your advisory council is no different.

CUSTOMER ADVISORY COUNCILS

An advisory council is a powerful tool that enables you to put a structured client input process in place to aid your product activities. Product managers form client councils to create a sounding board for proposed product activities. Advisory councils are typically made up of seven to nine clients who possess a keen insight into your market or the use of your product.

These councils serve two purposes. The first purpose is to *ensure thoughtful customer input into strategic or tactical product matters.* The scope of the conversation can range from evaluating a product roadmap to discussing a specific tactical decision that needs to be made from a range of possible options. Having insightful customers weigh in on the range of opportunities provides valuable input and buy-in. It can also provide a form of market validation that helps internally when product managers are faced with difficult or unpopular decisions.

The second purpose is to *help attract new clients.* Peer-to-peer client conversations regarding your product can be powerful. While prospects will often listen skeptically to a sales pitch, they are less inclined to disregard a peer's comment regarding their experience with your product. Members of your advisory council will often help trumpet your product in the market formally and informally.

Although these are both good reasons to form an advisory council, it can be a mistake to select advisory council members primarily for their ability to help in the sales process. Advisory councils work best when members have sufficient knowledge about your market and product to advise you on key product activities. That is the primary purpose that you form a council. Advisory councils often go awry when the outbound marketing purpose trumps the advisory mission of the group.

IDENTIFYING ADVISORY COUNCIL MEMBERS

Thankfully, you already have a good sense of where to look to find qualified candidates for your advisory council. During your earlier work, testing your product strategy and sharing your roadmap with various thought-leading clients, you were exposed to potential candidates. It is now time to sort through your mental inventory of these clients for those who fit your recruitment profile.

If you're forming a customer advisory council for the first time, or fine-tuning one that already exists, there are three things that you need to think through before reaching out to future members.

The first is what role or roles do you intend to include in your council? Will your group be made up of hands-on users, or do you want to incorporate the economic buyer who may not be the hands-on user? Perhaps you want to identify hands-on users who are also the economic buyers? Begin the process of identifying who you want to invite by answering the question of what role is best suited to help you achieve your objective now and in the future.

The second consideration is geographic distribution. It is often useful to have clients on the council who come from various regions of the country, or from various countries, depending on the span of your business. If we assume for a minute that your business is like Alpha Technology Ventures and serves the U.S., then you would ideally have customers from across the country. This serves two purposes: it provides insight into national market trends that may affect your business, and it will help with your sales and marketing activities because you'll have customer representatives in all regions.

The third consideration is related to each invitee's ability to contribute to the team. You're looking for individuals who are comfortable contributing in a team setting and will work collaboratively with you and their peers. Candidates who are too introverted to contribute to the overall flow of the discussion or too self-interested to collaborate with their peers make the work of an advisory council significantly harder. If possible, interview potential candidates either in person or by phone and get a sense of their interpersonal skills. Weeding out candidates that undermine the effectiveness of the group will pay dividends later.

If you do not have enough candidates, seek input from others inside your organization regarding people who meet the three criteria of role, geographic distribution, and teamwork. Once you've identified the best candidates for your council, go ahead and draw up a *charter document*.

What is an advisory council charter? It is a one-page document that outlines *your* expectations for participating members. It helps in several ways. You'll use it to make sure that your potential advisory members know what you expect *before* they join your council. It will also help you manage internal expectations. You'll be able to share the contents of the charter document with sales, marketing, engineering, and your senior leadership team.

Your advisory council charter should fit on one page and cover the following topics:

- Objective of the group
- Frequency of meetings
- Meeting duration
- Meeting location
- Participants in the council
- Timeframe

- Meeting dates and topics

- Other expectations

- Expenses

- Point person

Let's quickly walk through each of these.

Begin by outlining your objective for the group. For example, your objective might read something like this:

> *The objective of the Alpha Technology Ventures Advisory Council is to incorporate direct customer feedback into the development of our products and services. The council will work with product management to ensure that our organization prioritizes the appropriate capabilities into our product roadmap.*

Once the objective has been defined, communicate the frequency of meetings. This will vary based upon your needs and resources. However, once or twice a year is often sufficient. Also outline how long you anticipate the meeting will take. It is best to budget an entire day and, if possible, have clients come in the night before. You may want to take them out to dinner as a group to help build team chemistry and identify any issues of which you should be aware. Make sure to communicate where you intend to hold the meetings. Will you hold them at your headquarters? At a member's client site? Regardless of where you choose to hold the meeting, be sure to communicate your expectations.

Also outline who (what role or roles) you decided to include in the meetings. Will it be end-users, economic decision-makers, or perhaps a combination? Advisory councils are often viewed as prestigious, and the candidates you're soliciting will often want to know who their peers will be. The decisions you make regarding roster will likely impact who decides to join and who may pass.

You'll also need to define the term of each individual's participation in the group. It is best to specify a specific timeframe. One year is usually too short — members won't have enough time to build up good group chemistry. Remember, it's likely that you'll only meet once or twice a year. Two years often works well. Because evergreen tenures often create problems, be sure to clearly outline the term length when selecting new members. Include some language that lets you roll over any candidate that you choose. This will help with the continuity of the council over time and let you roll off candidates that may not have anything else to contribute.

Advisory council members are generally busy people. Make sure that you select your advisory council meeting dates well in advance. If you wait, you're likely to find that your members will already be booked. Publishing the dates in advance, *months in advance*, helps to ensure that you'll be able to hold your meeting. Also, publish the meeting topics to the clients before they arrive for the meeting, so they can review them beforehand.

Do you have other expectations for your advisory council members? It is not unusual to ask members for informal feedback at irregular intervals as you develop new product capabilities, or perhaps to have them act as test sites for your new products. If you want to interact with clients outside of the advisory council meetings, make sure to outline those expectations.

BE CAREFUL ABOUT CREATING THE PERCEPTION THAT ADVISORY COUNCIL TENURE IS EVERGREEN

Advisory council membership is often viewed as prestigious and customers enjoy engaging with their peers in active dialog on important topics. Properly managing expectations from the very beginning is critically important to prevent unintentionally undermining a strong relationship. Companies often create product advisory councils without clearly spelling out the tenure of the membership. These "evergreen" or never-expiring tenures often become problematic later on when the company changes focus, leadership, or direction. Make sure that tenure on the council is crystal clear to avoid problems down the road.

Another helpful area to address upfront is expenses. Explain how travel arrangements will be made and reimbursed. What is the process? Who will assist clients? Where should they go if they have questions? Also, explain expense policies. For example, will coach airfare be the norm or will you allow them to fly business class? Clarifying these points upfront will greatly reduce uncomfortable situations down the road.

Finally, explain who the point person is for the relationship between the advisory council members and your company going forward. Make sure that you share your contact information and ask permission to share theirs with the other members of the council.

SUPPORTING THE PRODUCT LAUNCH

Product launch represents the tail end of the product development process. Launching a product is a highly visible activity. The art of successfully bringing a product to market relies heavily on investing enough time *upfront* to ensure its success upon launch. This is the point where you communicate to the market what your product stands for and why customers should buy it. Once introduced to the market it is nearly impossible to pull a product back. The consequences, given the high visibility, are significant.

Let's begin our examination of product launch activities by first exploring how the nature of your market impacts what type of launch works best. There are three types of markets and two different approaches you can use.

The most common approach is focused on launching your product into an existing market. Existing markets typically have a number of dominant competitors all jockeying for market share. Launching into existing markets requires that you have a distinct value proposition that lets you stand out from the noise of the crowd and take as much market share from competitors as possible. Your launch plan needs to *single-mindedly focus on acquiring new customers and creating demand for your product.* As a result, your launch plan relies on an "all in" approach, using every available demand creation tool at your disposal to gain maximum attention over a specific timeframe. Given that you're leveraging all your available tools, this approach is expensive.

The second type of launch is geared toward new markets; in other words, markets that do not currently exist. In these markets you're investing for the long term and your objective is to *drive awareness and ultimately adoption of your product.* Because there are few, if any, customers for this offering, companies target early adopters to establish momentum and spark the interest of a currently uncaring mass market. Going "all in" at this point makes little sense, because there are not enough customers to justify the expense. Launching into this type of market is focused on attracting early adopters and educating the untapped market about your offering in the hopes of creating a tipping point.

The third type of market is resegmented. A resegmented market results from efforts to carve out a piece of an existing market by offering a lower-priced product than your competitors or by targeting a segment of the market that plays to your product or services strengths. With this type of market, your goal is to redefine the market conditions so you can target a winnable portion. Your objective is to both educate and capture market share. You'll need to choose between the two

WHAT IS A TIPPING POINT?

Tipping points are specific moments when the momentum of an idea or a product reaches critical mass and becomes mainstream. The concept of tipping points was introduced by Malcolm Gladwell in his book *The Tipping Point: How Little Things Can Make a Big Difference.*[2]

approaches listed above. If the segment of the market you're targeting is ready to buy, then consider the "all in" approach, if not, focus on attracting early adopters. Now that we have talked about how different market types impact your product launch strategy, let's discuss the activity of launching a product. Launching a product is a collaborative effort that involves a variety of cross-functional team members. One of the greatest challenges you face is coordinating the various aspects of the organization in support of the launch. This area rarely gets the attention it should, and it often shows in the launch results.

Once you know what type of launch style you'll use, it's helpful to create a product brief on the product or capability you're launching. The brief will outline the critical information regarding your value proposition, the customer audience you're targeting, and the key messages and channels you'll use to get your message out. This framework will help everyone involved.

NEW PRODUCT DEVELOPMENT METHODOLOGIES FURTHER CONSTRAIN THE PRODUCT LAUNCH PROCESSES

Although product development methodologies such as Agile — which focus on quick product releases and a high degree of iteration — are often very effective in producing results, organizations often underestimate the impact of these methodologies further downstream. Given the tight deadlines, technical writing, marketing, customer service, sales, and other parts of the organization often do not have enough time to get trained or complete their responsibilities before a release. Organizations need to think about *how all the pieces fit to optimize the entire system*, rather than just the engineering cycle, particularly as business grows.

The content in this brief will be created once and used many times. This document will enable your executive team to see your thought process and value proposition before the launch. Marketing will use the structured content you provide to professionally craft the message in their marketing plan and sales support materials; it will also help them select the right channels. Sales, channel partners, and customer service will benefit from the material as you train them for the launch.

What is a product brief? It is a one- to three-page document, created for all the stakeholders, that is the central information source about your new product or capability. It has the following sections:

- Product name and release date
- Who the product is targeted to
- Description of the product or capability
- Summary of the key customer business needs that the product or capability will address
- The customer value proposition
- Client impact
- Description of the launch plan and timing of key events
- Benefits and features
- Sales and customer service talking points
- Pricing
- Resources and additional information

Once complete, the product brief becomes the central source for maintaining consistent communication regarding the value of the product being launched. It helps keep internal team members on message. The product brief is not intended to be given to customers, but is used solely to provide internal team members the information they need to prepare for the launch.

Now that the key information has been defined, it is time to create a launch plan framework that helps coordinate the timing and tasks needed to successfully launch your product. Launch plan frameworks vary by business and level of complexity, so let's take a look at a basic template created in a spreadsheet format.

The best place to start developing your framework is to establish your launch date and work back from there. For example, if you plan to launch on October 1st, list the activities that need to take place before that date to determine when your plan needs to start. Once you know the launch date and the starting point, you can begin to fill in the blanks.

If you plan to start on June 1st and launch on October 1st, create a calendar that includes these dates and breaks time down into weekly increments over that time. Next create columns to list the task, owner, deliverable, target, and source of needed material. Once you have the columns created, list the activities in chronological sequence and fill in the owner through timeline columns. Your basic launch plan framework should look something like Figure 7. With your product strategy selected, product brief prepared, and your launch plan in hand, you and your counterparts are ready to focus on the tasks required for a successful launch.

FIGURE 7. LAUNCH PLAN FRAMEWORK

Alpha Technology Ventures Launch Plan - AlphaMobile

Launch Date 10/01

Task	Owner	Deliverable	Target	Source Material
Channel Partner Reference Card	Jack Moore	Channel template	USI Sales	PM, Sales, Marketing
Readiness Campaign begins	Sales/Marketing	Email/telephone	300 clients	Professional Services
Model Pricing	Sean Knight	Word document	CFO	Product Management
Direct mail campaign	Sales/Marketing	Email/telephone	300 clients	Product Management
AlphaMobile new business campaign	Sales/Marketing	Email/telephone	Prospects	Product Management
Complete product brief	Sean Knight	Word document	Marketing	Product Management
Product brief ready for use	Marketing	Word document	PM & Training	Product Management
AlphaMobile sell sheet developed	Marketing	Slick	Sales, PS, CS	Product Management
Internal training begins	Training Staff/PM	Training sessions	Sales, PS, CS	Product Management
Channel partner training begins	PM/Sales	Teleconference/site	USI Sales	Product Management
Meetings set up with clients	Sales	Various	Existing clients	Product Management
Meetings set up with prospects	Sales	Various	Prospects	Product Management
Beta's up and running	PM	Charter	TBD	Product Management
AlphaMobile contract developed	CM and Product Management	Contract	New/existing clients	Contract Management
AlphaMobile brochure ready	Marketing	Brochure	Sales, PS, CS	Product Management
AlphaMobile web pages ready	Marketing	Web page design	Sales, PS, CS	Product Management
External selling begins	Sales	Various	New/existing clients	Product Mgmt, Marketing
Product demos	Sales	Various	New/existing clients	Product Management

Timeline columns: June (6/3, 6/10, 6/17, 6/24), July (7/7, 7/14, 7/21, 7/28), August (8/5, 8/12, 8/19, 8/26), September (9/2, 9/9, 9/16, 9/23)

THE EMERGENCE OF AGILE

Software development teams have been adopting an approach — called Agile — that is radically different from the traditional Waterfall method we just discussed. Although this methodology has been around for some time, most companies are in the early stages of adopting it, and the evolution of Agile product management is at the back end of the learning curve. Because it often upends aspects of the existing processes and organizational structure, fully adopting Agile can take years and often requires a significant culture shift.

When product development organizations make a partial or total shift to Agile, product managers are often caught unawares. Typically the development team has been working to construct the staging for this change behind the scenes, and product management is alerted to the shift and the implications only after the basic infrastructure is in place. Product managers are often further confused by this change because the Agile methodology has its own vocabulary and often requires a different mindset and potentially a different configuration of skills.

Companies adopt Agile believing that it makes their organizations more responsive to changing market dynamics, helps cement better working relationships between the functional members of the value creation team, and increases the shared accountability for creating products and services. In many ways, the Agile framework is a reaction to the perceived inefficiencies that exist within the more traditional Waterfall methodology. These inefficiencies include onerous documentation, the slow pace of bringing features to market, and the assumption that the functional members of the value creation team will work together effectively for the common good and overcome awkward handoffs, rigid functional boundaries, and the lack of alignment that is often allowed to exist.

Agile, at its core, is intended to promote flexibility and adaptive behavior while enhancing collaboration within the team. Features are created and introduced to the market in quick release cycles known as *sprints*. Customers are actively included in these sprint cycles to enhance the product's value. Unlike the traditional development method, the timeframe for these small releases is typically one to four weeks, not months.

So what does Agile look like? The truth is, it varies from organization to organization. Although Agile is built upon a central philosophy and set of development methods, it must be adapted to each organization. Agile methods are generally characterized by close collaboration within the development team known as a *scrum*, frequent delivery of new releases in sprints, face-to-face communication with customers during the sprint, managed backlogs of user stories, self-organizing teams, and performance improvement self assessments.

Additionally, scrums share a common structure with three defined roles. The roles are *"product owner," "scrum master,"* and *"team member."* The product owner is first among equals and is the person that represents the customer within the team dynamic. While the product owner represents the customer, most of their time is actually focused on supporting the development team's needs for real-time input. This role requires full-time engagement with the scrum creating a prioritized backlog of features grouped into user stories, interpreting the product strategy, defining specifications, and feeding the development team with the necessary material to drive the development sprints and resolve any issues. This position is also known as the *"single wringable neck"* because this individual is vested with the final authority to make the critical decisions.

The scrum master's role on the team is to keep the team moving forward. This includes removing obstacles, planning sprints, and running daily "stand up" meetings that generally last about 15 minutes. The scrum master also runs reviews and retrospective meetings with a focus on continuously improving the team's productivity. The other members of the team contribute to the sprints — define, code, and test cycles.

Given Agile's radically different approach, the implications to you as a product manager are significant. To begin with, the roles of a product manager and a product owner are not synonymous! The breadth of your role as a product manager greatly exceeds the responsibilities of a product owner. The product owner's time is consumed supporting the needs of the scrum team. As a result, the product owner is not able to serve the larger strategic and broader market needs that your organization requires (defining markets, performing competitive analysis, setting pricing, designing packaging, etc.). In fact, losing sight of this broader strategic role can be catastrophic for your organization. Although Agile teams can often succeed on their own, doing market releases for a substantial period of time without strategic product input, eventually the lack of a broader market context risks undermining the overall market success of the effort and wasting resources.

Not every organization has the luxury of maintaining the strategic product manager role while adopting an Agile product development framework. But the risks of not doing so are significant! Ideally, the product owner should be incredibly detail-oriented and have strong analytic skills. Many organizations therefore choose business analysts, requirements analysts, or technical product managers to fill the product owner role. Having the product owner directly tied to the strategic product manager allows the former to represent the market-facing product manager. This ensures appropriate linkage with the market, while appropriately supporting the more feature-focused needs of the Agile product team.

Because their underlying tasks are so demanding, product owners can handle only two to three teams. The fast iteration cycles and the need to stay continuously engaged with the development team consume significant amounts of their time. The implication is that your organization might need to add resources to fill the product owner role as it converts to an Agile approach.

When Waterfall-oriented organizations adopt Agile methodologies, they take on significant challenges that are not quickly overcome. The main flash point, but not the only one, is the delineation of the product owner role with the existing role of product manager. The Agile methodology brings many benefits and is especially useful with less complex projects or when bringing new product capabilities to market. However, many organizations stick with the Waterfall method to handle more complex projects because it is more adroit at handling large-scale challenges. As a result, the best bet for many organizations is to blend both of these development methodologies to effectively serve their markets.

Finally, if your organization is in the process of adopting Agile, it is best that the team starts by taking small steps before engaging in full-scale Agile product design. If your organization has existing products, consider beginning your adoption of Agile by first tackling high priority defects as part of your maintenance process. Once your team finds a rhythm, expand your activity to encompass more complex projects. Keep in mind that just because you're following an Agile methodology doesn't mean you should release sprints to the market unless there is enough customer value to warrant doing so. Creating constant churn in your product without providing sufficient value to your customers can needlessly aggravate your client base. Carefully think through what constitutes a release.

AN ADDITIONAL COMMENT ON THE RISE OF AGILE METHODOLOGIES AND ITS IMPLICATIONS

The rapid rise in adoption of Agile product development methodologies means that product managers must become bilingual. Why? Industry data shows that the majority of organizations are blending Agile, typically scrum, with Waterfall. As a result, product managers and owners need to know both approaches to optimize their effectiveness and be able to comfortably shift their approach based upon company goals and objectives. This has become easier as product managers have become more accustomed to operating with a foot in both worlds but mastering both takes time.

CHAPTER SEVEN'S TIPS FOR TAKING CHARGE

- The core value creation team composed of product management, project management, and engineering need to share aligned performance-based objectives and incentives to maximize performance and function as a truly integrated group. When incentives are not aligned, each department will likely act to attain their specific goals at the expense of the team.

- Requirements documentation is "where the rubber meets the road." It is the part of the product development process where the engineering team translates your high-level market requirements into tangible capabilities. Be sure you and the engineering team agree on the template and the level of detail early in your tenure.

- A customer advisory council is a powerful tool that enables you to put a structured client input process in place to aid your product development activities. When forming a new council or revising an existing council, draft a charter document that outlines your expectations for participating members. This will clarify key points such as objectives, tenure, and expense reimbursement.

- Product launch is the final step of product development and is highly visible. Successfully bringing a product to market requires significant upfront planning and cross-functional collaboration. The most important element of a successful launch is understanding what type of market you're in. Once you determine your launch strategy, you'll need to develop a product brief and a tactical launch plan.

- Software development teams have been adopting an approach — called Agile — that is radically different from the traditional Waterfall method. If your organization is in the process of adopting Agile, it is best that the team starts by taking small steps before engaging in full-scale Agile product design. If your organization has existing products, consider beginning your adoption of Agile by first tackling high-priority defects as part of your maintenance process. Once your team finds a rhythm, expand your activity to encompass more complex projects.

CHAPTER EIGHT: NEVER TAKE YOUR EYES OFF THE MARKET

For the first time since I had taken the position 10 months ago, Robert Lamp was actually *sitting* at my desk. He had an anxious look.

Sinclair had just concluded the senior leadership team's bi-weekly staff meeting. He had informed Robert that he was "on point" to pull together detailed information on our market share and a thorough competitive analysis. Although Robert had often talked about both of these topics in meetings, his comments tended to be subjective and no one had fact-based metrics we could draw upon to definitively state our share and competitive position. What had made Robert even more anxious was that Kevin Knowles, our chairman of the board, was requesting a review of the information 30 days before the annual meeting, which meant Robert had less than 30 days to have *all* the information in Sinclair's hands.

Robert began our conversation in his usual jovial manner. "Sean, remember when I said you *owed* me one?" he said. "I faintly recall a conversation almost a year ago that went something like that," I answered coyly. Robert, looking a bit more hopeful, inquired, "Good, then I assume you'll help me pull together a competitive analysis for Sinclair?" Trying to hide my amusement at Robert's predicament, I responded, "Robert *when* is this analysis due to Sinclair?" Shifting a bit in his chair, he replied "in about three weeks." I decided to not let him off the hook too easily, and asked, "Which competitor do you want me to focus on?" With a look of dismay surfacing on his face, Robert quickly blurted out, "All of them!"

Realizing that he was now at a serious disadvantage and it was likely going to cost him, he offered some incentives to sweeten the deal. "Sean, if you're willing to do this for me, I'll take you out for drinks and you'll have a marker from me that you can use in the future. Do we have a deal?" he asked. Not realizing that Sinclair had already talked to me about helping Robert with the project — Sinclair viewed this as my domain anyway — I paused, considering his offer.

Willing to pay almost any price, Robert asked, "Okay, name it, what is it going to take?" Not wanting to have Robert get too anxious, I moved to close. "Alright, I'll help you," I said. "But you'll need to make it *dinner* and a marker." Looking like a balloon that was quickly re-inflating, Robert hopped out of my chair and vigorously shook my hand. "Deal!" he said. "Sean, I have to catch my flight, so I have to run, but let's talk about this next week, okay?" Before I could respond, Robert bounded out of the chair and like a hot air balloon, colorfully faded off into the horizon.

As I watched Robert head out, I couldn't help but laugh. I knew I wouldn't see him again until the project was complete!

MARKET DYNAMICS AND COMPETITIVE ANALYSIS FRAMEWORKS

Competitive analysis is the domain of product management. Although you'll likely be responsible for developing the frameworks for analyzing the competition, you'll be able to draw on information from a variety of sources to round out your view.

There are generally two vantages for competitive analysis: *point-in-time* and *near real-time*. Point-in-time analysis is a means of gathering currently available competitive information into a consolidated view. Most of the information will be retrospective, meaning publically available information that has been in the market for a period of time. Retrospective information is still useful and can be used to forecast where competitors are likely to go in the future.

The other form of competitive data gathering focuses on developing a cross-functional *system* that, while still retrospective, shortens the time lag and approximates near real-time. Sequentially, implementing a cross-functional data gathering process usually occurs *after* you've already developed point-in-time analysis and are looking to *stay in tune with your competitors' market movements*. To accomplish near real-time competitive analysis, you'll need to work with various functional counterparts, inside your organization, to develop a disciplined system for channeling competitors' market movements into product management.

Let's begin our conversation on competitive analysis frameworks with point-in-time analysis at the macro level.

MARKET VIEW — SEEING THE BIG PICTURE

It is often best to start by focusing in on the *overall market picture* before diving deeper into specific competitive threats. Some of the information we're going to talk about may already exist inside your organization with your senior leadership team or perhaps within marketing.

IT'S THE ONE YOU DIDN'T SEE COMING

When you're scanning the horizon for threatening competitors, it's important not to make assumptions. This will ensure that your thinking is not solely focused on your *known* competition. Experienced product managers will tell you that the competitor that snuck up on them, and hurt their business the most, was the unconventional one that was not on anybody's radar screen. Be sure to keep your eyes open for new competitors coming from promising start-ups, adjoining verticals, and large companies that can expand at will through partnerships or acquisitions.

So as we begin to frame up the "market view," keep in mind that some of this information is likely already available, although it may be dated.

Market view analysis generally includes a series of components:

- Market focus
- Size of your market and its anticipated growth rate
- Overview of your company's current market position
- Description of the market segments you serve
- Matrix of your top competitors by market segment
- More detailed breakdown of the competitors
- Overview of your current position with a focus on possible market opportunities
- Buy-versus-build opportunities
- Possible acquisition candidates
- List of risks and contingencies

- Potential competitive movements

- Deep dives into specific competitors

Let's walk through each of these components, using Sean's work as an example of how to create a presentation for your market view analysis. This exercise assumes that Alpha Technology Ventures serves the U.S. healthcare market.

The first component of your analysis, *market focus*, frames the specific market that your company is targeting. This sets the context for the other aspects of the analysis. Using our example of the healthcare market, Alpha Technology Ventures has decided to focus on business intelligence (BI) software solutions for U.S. hospitals. Therefore, Sean's analysis would visually illustrate all the components of a hospital's operations, including how patients are handled, diagnosed, and treated. It would then highlight those areas where Sean's business intelligence solutions create value for hospitals. In other words, it shows Alpha Technology Ventures target market — hospitals, the existing patient processes, *and where Sean's specific offerings add value.*

BUSINESS INTELLIGENCE

Business intelligence (BI) is a set of specialized software tools specifically designed to analyze business data contained in a data warehouse or a database system. These software tools strive to provide unique and actionable insights, distilled from raw data, to drive better decision making. Business intelligence tools are also commonly called decision-support applications for this very reason.

Next you must address market size and anticipated growth rate. Sean's second slide would detail how the segment he's targeting fits inside the overall U.S. healthcare market. If the U.S. healthcare market represents approximately $50 billion, the hospital segment Sean is targeting might represent $22 billion. The other $28 billion of the market consists of drug companies, insurance firms, and physicians. Each of these elements would have a dollar value associated with them as components of the overall market, and Sean would need to list each on the slide. Once complete, Sean would also need to list the projected annualized growth rate for each segment of the hospital market.

Now that Sean has framed his markets' size and growth rate, he'll need to explain where his company currently fits in. Is it the market leader? A contender or further back in the pack? Sean needs to list his company's market share and detail where

Alpha Technology Ventures fits into the context of competing companies that are all vying for a piece of the BI solutions market. For example, this market might only represent $3 billion of the $22 billion hospital market. Sean will need to list all the players and their representative market share.

If Sean's BI solutions cross multiple market segments inside hospitals, his target market, he will need to list these market segments next. Perhaps Alpha Technology Ventures provides BI solutions for hospital finance, clinical decision support, and client satisfaction. Each one of these is a different market segment.

Since Sean's company serves multiple market segments, like the three listed above, he will need to visually illustrate the top competitors by market segment. The range of competitors might be few in a new market segment or numerous in a growing market.

Next, Sean needs to create a slide that shows the top competitors and describes how they compete with his organization. Do they only impact one market segment or do they compete across multiple dimensions of the business? Sean's slide will list competitors on the left and have a series of columns that show their revenue and the market segments that they play in.

Once complete, Sean will need to detail the top five competitors and prepare a short narrative describing each company's profile, strategic direction, and partnerships. The profile paragraph should outline each company's primary focus and what differentiates their market approach from competitors. The strategic direction segment should attempt to outline their known strategy and where Sean thinks the company is headed. Key partners or relationships might outline channel relationships, associations, or partners that provide your competitors with a leg up in the market. Sean will then focus on his company's position in the market in relation to the competition. He will need to describe his company's core capabilities. What are the core gaps that need to be filled? What segment-level opportunities exist that he could capitalize on?

With a solid understanding of the macro position of each competitor, his company's relative position in the market, and a solid understanding of the gaps in his offering, Sean can begin to record his thoughts about buy-versus-build scenarios that strengthen his products' competitive position. Sean will outline each of the gaps he thinks he needs to focus on and the relative strength or weakness of his current position. He will also frame whether he thinks it's better to buy or build certain aspects of his products' future capabilities.

If Sean is now convinced it's better to acquire than build a component of his offering, he will need to create a list of acquisition targets over the short and long-term to shore up his competitive position. Assuming his company has the capital to invest and the skill to integrate acquisitions, he will need to list his target companies, their revenue, and the market segment or segments they serve.

BUY VERSUS BUILD

As a product manager, you'll eventually make a buy-versus-build decision. Although the criteria for your decision will vary based on your industry and business, there are some general things to consider. First, make sure that you have very *clearly defined business needs*. If your business needs are not well understood, you're headed for trouble! It's not uncommon to find that your organization has short-, medium-, and long-term needs. To start, create a way to capture these needs and rank them high, medium, or low. Once you're comfortable that you've accurately captured the full range of needs, make sure you consider timing, costs, value-added capabilities, and the culture of any organization that you consider acquiring. If your organization prides itself on fast customer support and your acquisition target does not, your business can face negative consequences. Make sure you also document risks and assumptions.

Sean will then detail any known risks associated with his buy recommendation. For example, is it clear how his target company should be valued? If not, that is a significant risk. Spell out any contingency plans. What happens if a preferred target is not open to being acquired? What is the next step? Will Sean pursue organic development of this capability, look at other acquisition targets, etc.?

He will then need to frame competitive market movements. Has one of his competitors been on an acquisition binge lately? Has it just raised capital? Is it trying to control strategic channels important to Sean's business? Sean will need to list any anticipated competitive responses to Alpha Technology Ventures' future strategic moves.

The final element of Sean's overall market view is to dive deeper into the profile of his top five competitors. He will need to create a quick summary of each competitor, their annual revenue, number of employees, their ownership status, their products, and any conclusion he has come to regarding their direction.

This market view is extremely helpful in keeping everyone at the senior leadership level aligned around the market you currently serve, the market segments you want to grow, your plan on achieving growth, and your top competitors' roles in the market. However, this type of analysis is not generally shared with other elements of the company, so *you'll need to develop a different framework for your customer-facing counterparts* in the organization.

NARRATIVE COMPETITIVE ANALYSIS

The information contained in your macro analysis is too sensitive and strategically important to share with the majority of your organization. Functional areas that deal with the sales process and client support will need another form of competitive analysis. One method to help train your customer-facing teams on competitor capabilities is to build more detailed competitive profiles specifically for their use.

The more your customer-facing team members know about your competitors, the more able they are to overcome objections and move the sales process forward with clients. Building a point-in-time competitor profile that can be used with customer-facing teams is often very helpful. As your organization grows, it will add team members who may have come from another industry or perhaps even from college. Moreover, developing and maintaining competitive profiles that can be used to quickly get new team members up to speed can often be invaluable.

Let's look at a standard point-in-time narrative competitive profile. Each competitor's profile would outline the following components:

- Name of the competitor
- Organizational history
- Business model and revenues
- Mission
- Vision
- Strategy
- Estimated client levels (overall and by product)
- Partnerships
- Positioning

- Detailed analysis of product/service offerings and stated benefits

- Pricing

- Recent developments

SALES PROCESS

Companies implement a systematic, repeatable sales process to scale revenue more quickly. Sales processes follow a series of well-defined steps intended to result in a successful sale. The ultimate goal of any sales process is to secure new business for your company while establishing positive rapport with the client. While sales processes vary from one company to another, most models share similar components. These include: prospecting, qualifying, making a proposal, negotiating, and closing.

Although it is time consuming to pull together, an amazing amount of competitive information is available via company annual reports, Hoovers (a source for business information on industries, companies, and corporate executives), company websites, press releases, articles, social networking sites, win/loss analysis, and other various sources. You'll find it relatively easy to gather information — now that you know where to look.

Let's quickly walk through this framework. Begin with the company's history. When was it founded? How does the company describe itself? How has it changed since inception? This type of information is generally available in annual reports and on the company website.

Next detail the business model. What type of company is it? Is it privately held or public? Do you compete against a division of a larger organization or are they solely focused on your market? What do you know about their annual revenue? If this competitor is publicly held, revenue information will be easier to source than if they are private.

What is the company's mission? You'll often find this on their company website. Company vision statements can be very insightful. What is their vision focused on? How wide ranging is it? What does it imply? How is it different from where they stand today? Do they describe the steps they intend to take to achieve their vision? How long is their line of sight — three, five, or perhaps 10 years?

Does the company communicate its strategy? It's not uncommon to find that companies will outline their strategy in investor presentations, on their website, or even in press releases.

DON'T OVERLOOK INVESTOR PRESENTATIONS

Companies often post investor presentations or transcripts of these presentations on their corporate websites. Investor presentations can be a rich source of competitive information. It is not uncommon for company executives to overview sales by market segment, their geographic reach, key financial metrics, their current and future market strategies, growth drivers, and any upcoming product launches.

What does your competitor say about their client numbers by market, segment, and product? This information is often available in the public domain although the methods competitors use to calculate this data often lead to inflated or hazy customer counts. Make sure to do a gut check if the numbers seem off, and make note of their list of key customers.

All partnerships are not created equally. What partners do your competitors tout? What type of partners are they — strategic, channel, marketing relationship, etc.? *Try to determine what need these partners are filling*; it will also tell you a great deal about what the company sees as its own weaknesses.

How does the company position itself? How are the products positioned? Describe each product or service and its relative positioning in as much detail as possible, succinctly. Remember, your counterparts in the client-facing parts of the organization will be interested in this information.

Now detail what you know about each product. What are its capabilities? What are the stated benefits they trumpet? What components, features, and functions differentiate it from your own? What are your relative strengths and weaknesses compared with the competitor? What have you learned that might help you overcome objections in the sales process?

Outline what you know about your competitors' pricing. It is not uncommon for customers to hint at or tell you competitors' pricing or to find information about competitors' pricing schemes in the public domain. Remember, it is exceptionally risky to use pricing information that came from a source other than the public domain, since you'll incur the risk of a lawsuit. Pricing information is very sensitive and companies rightly guard this information with every means possible.

Finally, have there been any recent developments at the competitor? Perhaps they have announced a new CEO and new strategy? Maybe they just spun off a division or acquired a new company? Did they just announce a new product or target a new market segment? By building a profile for each of your key competitors, you've helped your company's customer-facing teams become more effective. Now that you have the information, you need to decide how to best put it to use.

> ## LEGAL REVIEW
> To minimize any legal risk, it is wise to have your legal team review any competitive analysis you've completed *before* making it available to your customer-facing teams. No matter how hard you try to keep this information from leaving your organization and reaching the market, it inevitably will.

It is often best to incorporate this data into specific training regimes. Whether you choose to do this via meetings, conference calls, or another type of format will depend on the geographic distribution of your organization and your company's culture. In smaller organizations, face-to-face meetings work the best. In a larger organization, other means are often required. Don't forget to post relevant information behind your company firewall on a marketing intranet site or some other secure central repository so new employees or team members with specific needs have access to the information.

Before posting any information, you'll need to reinforce to your customer-facing teams that competitive information is *not to be distributed to anyone outside of the organization*. It is intended for internal training purposes only. Put a disclaimer on each of these profiles marking them confidential and for internal use only.

Disseminating this information works best when it is jointly presented with a cross-functional team member who can *relate personal anecdotes that bring the competitive information to life*. This seems to help the customer-facing teams relate to the information. Choose whichever format works best for your organization; my personal preference is to co-present this information in a meeting with a member of the customer-facing team.

One final note: if you decide to stop at point-in-time analysis, you'll need to update the data at least annually.

DEVELOP A SYSTEM TO CAPTURE NEAR REAL-TIME MARKET INFORMATION

It is virtually impossible to collect information on competitive movements in real-time; however, it is possible to capture competitive information in *near* real-time. This will require that your organization makes a concerted effort to collect and channel market information to a central point — product management for aggregation and analysis. By implementing a cross-functional market intelligence system, you can often narrow the lag time to see market movements as quickly as possible.

DON'T REINVENT THE WHEEL!

It is best if you can leverage an existing format for collecting market data. For example, the sales team may have to submit a bi-weekly sales report to the organization and sales leadership. If you can get sales to add a paragraph about competitor activities to this report, so much the better. Ask the other customer-facing aspects of the organization to follow the same format to reduce complexity.

Reach out to the leaders in sales, consulting, customer service, and the executive team — anyone who interacts with clients directly — and gain agreement on a format for submitting market intelligence back to product management for analysis. To achieve this you'll need to gain agreement, with all involved, on a *short format* that allows each contributor to channel data back to you in a usable form. The shorter the format, the better — everyone is busy. To optimize participation, you'll want to minimize the time submitters need to spend on sending you intelligence.

To keep the system going, you'll need to analyze the incoming information and send updates to all the parties involved. This positively reinforces the value of submitting the information in the first place and helps the customer teams increase their knowledge and ultimately results.

Depending on the resources available to you, you may want to consider using recognition and rewards to reinforce the importance of submitting competitive information. Work with your senior leadership team to develop an incentive system to keep the information flowing. This might include gift cards, dinner with a member of the senior leadership team, or some other incentive.

Once the system is established and becomes an expectation, you're well on your way to having your eye firmly affixed to your market.

CHAPTER EIGHT'S TIPS FOR TAKING CHARGE

- There are generally two vantages for competitive analysis; *point-in-time* and *near real-time*. Point-in-time analysis is a means of gathering existing competitive information into a consolidated view. This contrasts with near real-time competitive data gathering, which focuses on developing a cross-functional *system* that, while still retrospective, shortens the time lag and enables your organization to stay in tune with competitors' market movements.

- Begin your competitive analysis at the macro level, focusing on your overall view of the market. Once complete, you'll find this information extremely helpful in keeping everyone at the senior leadership team level aligned around the dynamics of the market you currently serve, the market segments you want to grow, your plan on achieving growth, and the role your competitors play.

- The information in your macro-level analysis is too sensitive and strategically important to share with most of your organization. Client-facing teams will require a more granular form of competitive analysis. Build detailed competitive profiles for your key competitors that can make your counterparts more knowledgeable about overcoming competitive challenges and enable new team members to quickly come up to speed on the competitive playing field.

- Although it is virtually impossible to collect competitive information in real-time, it is possible to implement a near real-time market intelligence collection system. This will require a concerted cross-functional effort to channel intelligence into a central collection point — product management — for analysis and dissemination.

CHAPTER NINE: DOCUMENTING RESULTS

The last three weeks had been the most stressful of my career. Sinclair had put the entire leadership team through their paces preparing, and then continually rehearsing, for tomorrow's annual management team review with the board. I had been included in all the preparations, and Sinclair had made it clear that my presentation was one of the most anticipated components of the meeting.

My lack of familiarity with the board members was making me very nervous. But as that feeling seeped into my core, I shook it off, and stared once more at a list of all that I had accomplished over the last 12 months. I have to admit I was particularly proud of my accomplishments. I had made a short list of the tangible items I had put into place since assuming the product manager role, and it was surprisingly extensive! I decided to look at the list one more time, before leaving for our dinner with the board, to bolster my confidence:

- ☑ Influence map
- ☑ Stakeholder surveys (the original and one I had just completed two weeks ago)
- ☑ Three-year product strategy
- ☑ Defined product milestones
- ☑ Business case
- ☑ Product lifecycle management framework
- ☑ Product decision matrix
- ☑ Rolling product roadmaps — internal and external

☑ Our shared goals (product management, project management, and engineering)

☑ New requirements documentation

☑ Advisory council and charter

☑ Product launch plan

☑ Competitive analysis (market view and narrative)

The list was nearly complete; however, I was just putting the finishing touches on my *new product scorecard* and n*ext year's product management activities calendar*. There would soon be two more items to add to the list!

Sinclair and the majority of the leadership team had been tremendously supportive throughout my tenure as a product manager. However, they were even more supportive when they grasped how much had been accomplished. Most of these product management deliverables did not exist before I took on my new role, and our execution had increased significantly after their implementation. We were still not hitting 80 percent of our customer-facing releases, but we were now running at almost 70 percent on time, on budget, and on scope and trending in the right direction. It would probably take another six months before we hit our goal, but we were well on our way.

The work I had completed over the last year had resulted in a clear vision of the future: the steps we needed to take on the path to attaining our market goals and a detailed understanding of where we stood relative to our competition. The ball was in our court to execute the plan and to remain alert to any changes in our markets' dynamics.

Sinclair had shared my presentation with Kevin Knowles, our chairman, and his feedback had been positive. Kevin told Sinclair that he thought the rest of the board would also appreciate what had been accomplished and its implications for the overall direction of the business. I don't think that Sinclair had been worried, but *I had been relieved* to learn of Kevin's comments. My presentation to the board tomorrow would cover the following topics:

- A walk-through of our market, our share, and our competitive environment

- A financial overview of my product and its current rate of growth

- Our new three-year product strategy

- Review of our last 12 months of product releases

- An overview of our newly deployed product lifecycle management process

- Product roadmap plans for the next 12 months

- A review of product management's goals for the year and where we finished

- Next steps and conclusion

Glancing at my watch, I realized it was time to leave. As I reached for my jacket, Robert poked his head around the corner and asked, "So, are you ready to go?" As I donned my jacket, I turned to Robert, smiled, and replied, "Thanks for driving, Robert." Robert chuckled and said, "My pleasure Sean, after all *I promised to take you to dinner* didn't I?"

OBJECTIVE DATA IS ESSENTIAL FOR YOUR SUCCESS

As a product manager, you'll need to rely heavily on objective data. Everyone has opinions; few have facts. Facts are concrete and often immutable. Objective facts neutralize opinions and provide the fuel that enables you to establish yourself as *the* market expert that everyone relies on.

Facts are not only useful in establishing your credibility, they are essential for communicating what you've accomplished. You'll need to develop a framework for quantifying your success.

As we will see, one of the most effective means of doing so is to develop a product scorecard. While quantitative data is central to your success, you cannot afford to overlook the qualitative dimension of product management. Product managers are in highly visible positions that rely heavily on influence and interpersonal skills. Given the high visibility, a lot is expected of you. As you move up the leadership curve, you're judged not only on *what* you've accomplished (the facts) but *how* you've achieved your objective (subjective perceptions). Both dimensions need to be effectively managed for you to be successful. Let's explore both of these dimensions in more detail.

INTERNAL METRICS OF SUCCESS

When you initially assumed your role, one of the first steps you took was to ask for a copy of your company's business plan. The business plan contained a wealth of information that helped you come up the learning curve quickly. Contained within the business plan were financial projections regarding the rate of revenue growth for the company and your product. These financial metrics and assumptions are often translated into the financial metrics that become a component of your annual performance goals.

If your company's business plan was to grow your products' revenue by $1,000,000 over the year, you probably have this as a personal goal. You'll also have several more goals, like the ones Beth, Sean, and Alex proposed to Sinclair. The goals you agreed on with your senior leadership team are one of the primary ways your organization measures your personal success.

We know four of Sean's goals:

- Achieve the company's sales and margin targets
- Publish fully resourced product roadmaps
- Achieve 80 percent of customer-facing roadmap deliverables (defined as on time, on scope, and on budget)
- 100 percent compliance with the product lifecycle management process

It is relatively easy to determine whether Sean and the team met their goals. For example, they either did or did not publish fully resourced product roadmaps and deliver 100 percent compliance with the product lifecycle management process. Sean is also able to track his team's progress toward the 80 percent performance goal for customer-facing deliverables by monitoring roadmap execution (we know they improved to approximately 70 percent).

MANAGING WITH A PRODUCT SCORECARD

While finance can determine whether Sean achieved the company's sales and margin targets for his product, he has decided to take a more hands-on approach. He has worked with finance to create a product scorecard that allows him to track monthly progress toward his financial targets. He created this tool so he could intervene throughout the year when circumstances warrant and to document his year-end results. Let's take a closer look at his product scorecard in Figure 9.

Across the top of Sean's product scorecard, there are several column headers:

- The full year's *actual* performance

- The full year's *budgeted* performance
- *Monthly* numbers for the current and previous years (actual and budgeted)
- *Year-to-date* numbers for the current year, against this year's budget and the previous year's actual

The column that runs down the left side of the scorecard contains the specific metrics that Sean wants to track:

- Pipeline
- Customer count
- Annualized subscription value
- Number of contracts up for renewal
- Value of the contracts up for renewal
- Number of customers that renewed
- Early renewal count
- Total dollars renewed
- Revenue renewal rate
- Number of new customers
- Dollar value
- Contract length
- One-time sales
- Number of customers implemented
- Average number of days to implement

Sean is now able to track a wide variety of financial metrics that will impact his ability to achieve his financial goals. By monitoring critical aspects of his products' success, he can work with the appropriate functions, within the organization, to investigate identified problems and seek alternative solutions that allow him to keep his revenue and margin goals on track.

FIGURE 9. PRODUCT SCORECARD FRAMEWORK

METRICS	Prior Year Actual	This Year's Budget	This Year's Actual Month	This Year's Budget Month	Last Year's Actual Month	This Year's Actual YTD	This Year's Budget YTD	Last Year's Actual YTD
Product Book Metrics								
Pipeline above 50%								
# of customers		8	19					
Amt of annualized subscription value		84,000	266,870					
Active Customer Book								
# of customers	356	411	380	NA	NA	380	NA	NA
Revenue	$3,809,000	$4,784,000	433,097	425,700	$323,406	$2,798,119	$2,734,206	2,132,097
Customer Book up for Renewal								
# of contracts	397	55	3	0	16	43	46	366
Value of contracts	$2,275	$485	$35	$0	$137	$345	$376	$2,231
Product Sales Metrics								
Renewals								
(a) # of customers who renewed	397	55	3	0	16	43	46	366
(b) Early renewal count	0	0	0	0	0			
(c) Scheduled renewal count (a)-(b)	397	55	3	0	16	43	46	366
(d) Customers up for renewal	397	55	3	0	16	43	46	366
Customer Renewal Rate (c)/(d)	100%	100%	100%		100%	100%	100%	100%
(a) Total $ renewed	$2,679	$443	$35		$137	$345	$376	$2,231
(b) Early $ renewed	$0	$0				$39	$0	$25
(c) Scheduled $ renewed (a)-(b)	$2,679	$443	$35	$0	$137	$306	$376	$2,206
(d) Contract amt. up for renewal	$2,275	$485	$35	$0	$137	$393	$393	$2,233
Revenue Renewal Rate (c)/(d)	118%	91%				78%	96%	99%
New Sales								
# of customers	58	29	1	1	35	12	12	49
Amt of subscription sales	$840	$400	$20	$14	$14	$13	$14	$14
Avg contract length (in years)	3	NA	3	NA	NA	NA	NA	NA
Amt of one-time sales	$153	$0	$78,120	$0	$0	$178,120	$0	$62
One-Time Sales								
# of customers	86	0	33	0	0	49	0	
Amt of one-time sales	$153	$0	$78,120	$0	$0	$178,120	$0	$62
Product Support / Operations Metrics								
Customer Support								
# of customers implemented	20		5			18		
Avg days to implement	14.3		122			79.5		
# of entries	335		11			113		
# of customer issues opened	4,937		566			3364		
# of customer issues closed	4,932		562			2944		

While these metrics work for Sean, you'll need to work with your finance team to develop meaningful metrics for your product and translate them into a scorecard that allows you to quantitatively monitor progress toward your financial goals. Product scorecards are also a handy way to review progress-to-date with your senior leadership team, and they help you understand the mechanisms that drive your product's success or failure.

AUTOMATED METRICS WORK BEST

As you begin to create your product scorecard, you'll often discover that some metrics can only be calculated manually. Rather than focusing on these manual metrics, first concentrate on capturing the metrics that can be automatically populated. This will allow you to get most of your scorecard in place and begin the active management of your product. Once the more accessible metrics are in place, you can work with finance to determine whether the manual metrics are valuable enough to invest in automating.

The quantitative metrics of success are only one-half of the equation. *How* you achieve your results also matters. Organizations have a variety of channels to communicate your interpersonal effectiveness. Performance reviews, informal mentoring, one-on-one discussions with the person you report to, and the way people react to you all provide insight into your effectiveness.

It is possible for someone to succeed on the metrics dimension of product management and still fail as a product manager. So, gauging how you're perceived is very important. Keep your radar on and read your environment. Be sure to *proactively seek feedback*. Remember, feedback is most painful when it has been building for a long time, so seek out feedback regularly in an effort to continually improve your performance. Don't wait until it has to hit you between the eyes. By then it is usually too late.

One final thought on gauging your effectiveness on more subjective grounds: the stakeholder survey that you implemented shortly after you took the role provides a baseline for you to compare how you're being perceived. Sean had recently sent out the survey for a second time to see what everyone thought about his efforts and the direction he has taken. Surveys can often reveal whether interpersonal "speed bumps" are impacting others' perceptions of your effectiveness. If you do identify any issues, take the time to privately speak to the other party and listen to their perspective.

Remain objective; if you believe your behavior is responsible for creating unflattering perceptions, work to make the appropriate changes.

SOMETIMES PERCEPTIONS ISSUES ARE UNAVOIDABLE

In certain instances it is unavoidable to ruffle some feathers or perceptions. For instance, you may be asked to review pending contracts with representatives from finance and sales to ensure the optimal financial return to your organization. The deal you're reviewing may generally be a good one, but rather than ask for a cost of living increase, which is standard in your contracts, the sales person may have avoided it so he could close the deal more quickly and make his quarterly sales quota. You and the finance representative may see the COLA clause as necessary. As a result, the sales person is sure to be quite unhappy about having to go back and add the cost of living increase. These types of instances are often unavoidable.

EXTERNAL METRICS OF SUCCESS

The internal measures of success, both quantitative and perception-orientated, are important ways for you to understand how effective you are as a product manager. *The external metrics of success illustrate what customers think about your company's effectiveness.*

Quantitatively, customers will measure your organization's success against what you promised to deliver on your customer-facing roadmap. There are two dimensions to this commitment. The first relates to the decisions you made regarding *which capabilities* made it onto your customer-facing roadmap. The second element is whether you *released the promised capability or product when you said you would.* Roadmaps are viewed by clients as *commitments*, and they will judge your efforts accordingly.

If you succeed in selecting the right products or capabilities and successfully deliver against your commitments, most customers will view your results positively. However, if you release products or capabilities that miss the mark, miss the promised release window, or deliver reduced capabilities or inferior quality, you'll create high levels of customer dissatisfaction. Compounding these errors over time rapidly undermines customers' trust in your organization.

It is not always apparent, on the surface of your metrics, that customers *feel* this way; the greatest proportion of your customers are likely a *silent* majority. They may be looking for other options and biding their time. Therefore, it is important to conduct satisfaction surveys to learn their perceptions.

Customer satisfaction surveys are useful tools that can help you understand the health of your customer base and measure how customers perceive the effectiveness of your organization. If your organization has continued to miss product release windows and reduce the amount of capability you deliver to clients, you'll likely learn that your customers perceive your organization as ineffective. Perpetuated over time, these execution errors will encourage your clients to seek other alternatives.

Customer satisfaction can also shine light on other dimensions of your customers' perceptions, such as the quality of your sales interactions, the effectiveness of your customer support, and product quality.

Knowing what customers think about your organization and your product efforts provides you with an opportunity to make needed adjustments.

MAKE THE SHIFT TO PROACTIVE PRODUCT MANAGEMENT

One of the chief indicators of a truly successful product management organization, other than market success, is its ability to move from being reactive to proactive. This is accomplished by putting the appropriate level of process in place and ensuring that everyone understands their roles and what to expect.

Oddly enough, many product organizations never reach this proactive state. There is nothing worse, as a product manager, than being continually buffeted around without the ability to seize the reins and bring order to your product. If you think about it, predictability is highly valued in just about every aspect of the organization. The leadership team wants to deliver predictable results to the investment community. Sales wants to deliver the predicted amounts of revenue. The leadership team and sales are both rewarded handsomely when this occurs.

INTRODUCE A PRODUCT MANAGEMENT CALENDAR

Once the baseline processes have been established, cross the threshold from being reactive to being proactive by putting into place a *product management calendar of events*. By proactively communicating the *internal* timetable for key events essential for your team's success, you're letting everyone know what to expect in advance. Most importantly, you're taking control. Putting out a product management calendar of events allows you to manage your workflow and your schedule.

Sean's calendar lists the following events:

- Roadmap publishing dates

- Roadmap iteration meeting dates

- Advisory group meetings

- Cross-functional team meetings

- Client conference dates

- Sales conference dates

- Product pricing submission dates to finance

- Product training dates for the customer-facing teams

- Budget and forecasting due dates

- Annual board meeting date

Publishing a calendar requires more thought than it might appear at first glance. Many of the events that need to occur have to happen in a particular order, and your business may have a certain sales cycle that you're attempting to synchronize your releases around. Carefully think through the various dimensions of your activities before publishing your calendar.

LEAVING DOCUMENTATION BEHIND FOR THOSE WHO FOLLOW

Now that Sean has created a comprehensive set of product management materials and contributed content to a wide variety of sales and marketing collateral, he needs to think about creating a centralized repository for these materials.

One of the facts of life in product management is that when you step into the role you rarely find a comprehensive set of materials that enable you to fully understand what was done before you assumed the role. This is true in organizations like Alpha Technology Ventures where no one was "officially" in the role before Sean's promotion, and it also holds true in mid-sized companies and more mature organizations.

Many a product manager walked into his new role and found little or no useful information. So once you've gotten to the point where you're in control, invest some time in assembling materials for the product manager that follows in your wake.

Here is a quick checklist of product management materials for you to include in a central repository:

- ☑ Stakeholder surveys
- ☑ Three-year product strategy
- ☑ Defined product milestones
- ☑ Business case
- ☑ Product lifecycle management framework
- ☑ Product decision matrix
- ☑ Rolling product roadmaps — internal and external
- ☑ Requirements documentation
- ☑ Advisory council members and charter
- ☑ Product launch plans
- ☑ Competitive analysis (market view and narrative)
- ☑ Copies of your product scorecard
- ☑ Your product management calendar
- ☑ Marketing collateral
- ☑ Presentations
- ☑ Customer satisfaction information
- ☑ Market research
- ☑ Win/loss data
- ☑ Customer proposal templates
- ☑ Pricing information
- ☑ Budget information
- ☑ Training materials
- ☑ Marketing plans
- ☑ Any other useful information

HARD WORK PAYS OFF

After reviewing all the work Sean has completed, it is very clear that *he really does have a tremendous amount to be proud of.* Over the last 12 months he has demonstrated the ability to conduct thoughtful research, carve out a position based on facts, and understand his market and competitors better than anyone else in the organization.

These skills have effectively established Sean as *the* go-to person for his organization in terms of understanding market requirements and translating market needs into valuable products and services. As you follow a similar path, others will turn to you for both leadership and direction. Once they do you'll have successfully made the transition into product management!

CHAPTER NINE'S TIPS FOR TAKING CHARGE

- Objective data and facts neutralize opinions and provide the fuel that enables you to establish yourself as *the* market expert that everyone relies on. Facts are not only useful in establishing your credibility, they are essential for communicating what you've accomplished.

- Although quantitative data is central to your success, you cannot overlook the qualitative dimension of product management. Product managers are in highly visible positions that rely heavily on influence and interpersonal skills. Given the high visibility, a lot is expected of you. As you move up the leadership curve, you'll be judged not only on *what* you've accomplished but *how* you've achieved your objectives. Both dimensions need to be effectively managed for you to be successful.

- A *product scorecard* is a useful quantitative tool that enables you to adopt a hands-on approach and monitor the trajectory of your product *each month.* Work with finance to develop the appropriate metrics. Once established, your product scorecard will provide you the opportunity to intervene when circumstances warrant.

- Cross the threshold from being reactive to proactive by implementing a *product management calendar of events.* By proactively communicating the timetable for key events that are essential for your team's success, you're letting everyone know what to expect in advance. Most importantly, you're taking control. This also allows you to proactively manage your workflow and schedule.

- One of the facts of life in product management is that when you step into the role you rarely find a comprehensive set of materials that allow you to fully understand what was done *before* you assumed the role. Once you've gotten to the point where you're in charge, invest some time in assembling materials for the next product manager.

EPILOGUE

The day after the board meeting, Sinclair called me to his office for a debriefing of my participation in yesterday's board meeting. I was confident that the meeting had gone well, and as I walked into Sinclair's office I reflected on how smoothly things had gone. Clearly all the work we had done, the preparation that Sinclair had put everyone through, and the cohesiveness that the team demonstrated in front of the board had paid dividends.

As I sat down in Sinclair's office, he walked to his table with a printed email in his hand. He settled into his chair and passed the email to me without a word, but with a smile in his eyes. Without hesitation, I absorbed the email:

Beaming from ear to ear, I set the email down and savored the moment.

✉ Reply ✉ Reply All ✉ Forward

Kevin Knowles | Sinclair Jones
Congratulations on Another Successful Meeting   ⌄

Sinclair,
I want to thank you for what the board members viewed as a very successful meeting with your leadership team. The information the team presented and the degree of preparation was exceptional. The board recognizes the amount of effort you put into the meeting. Great job!

I also want you to pass along our thanks to Sean for his product management presentation. We see why you have so much confidence in him. After the meeting with your team, the board met in closed session and revisited our previous discussion about the value of product management. Everyone clearly understands this value now. It's like I've always said, "you know it when you see it." We've come a long way.

Kevin

REFERENCES

[1]Ulwick, Anthony. *What Customers Want: Using Outcome-Driven Innovation to Create Breakthrough Products and Services.* New York: McGraw-Hill, 2005.

[2]Gladwell, Malcolm. *The Tipping Point: How Little Things Can Make a Big Difference.* New York: Back Bay Books, 2002.

INDEX

ABOUT THE AUTHOR

Greg Geracie is a recognized thought leader in the field of product management and the President of Actuation Consulting, the world's leading product management consulting and training organization. Actuation Consulting is a global provider of product management consulting, training, and advisory services to many of world's most well-known organizations.

Greg is the author of two global best sellers *Take Charge Product Management* and *The Guide to the Product Management and Marketing Body of Knowledge.* He is also an adjunct professor at DePaul University's College of Computing and Digital Media where he teaches graduate and undergraduate courses on high-tech and digital product management.

Greg is a former board member of the Business Architecture Guild where he contributed to the most recent version of the BIZBOK Guide. As an industry expert, Greg has also been asked to contribute his product management expertise to a growing list of professional bodies of knowledge, including the Institute of Electrical and Electronics Engineers (IEEE) first ITBOK and the latest BABOK Guide. Greg is currently a member of the IEEE's Information Technology Committee.

Greg earned his undergraduate degree from the University of Vermont and continued his executive education at Harvard University, the Massachusetts Institute of Technology (MIT), and the Wharton School.

You can learn more about Greg and Actuation Consulting at ActuationConsulting.com.

ABOUT ACTUATION CONSULTING

Actuation Consulting provides professional product management consulting and training to leading organizations worldwide. Visit ActuationConsulting.com.

PRODUCT MANAGEMENT TRAINING

Organizations often struggle to utilize a common vocabulary and implement effective and sustainable processes. Our product management training courses help organizations address these issues and create meaningful change to improve product team performance.

- *Take Charge Product Management* for Product Professionals – Expert training for your product team based on the principles and leading techniques discussed in *this book*!
- Software and Digital Media Product Management
- Training for Product and Project Managers – Creating Value Through Collaboration
- An Introduction to Product Management for Product Team Members

PRODUCT MANAGEMENT CONSULTING

Our full range of product management services ranges from interim product management leadership to helping your team address a particular business challenge.

- Professional Assessment Services
- Product Management Advisory Services
- Onsite Product Management Consulting

PRODUCT AND PROJECT MANAGEMENT TOOLKITS

Hit the ground running with our easy-to-use product and project management templates and toolkits.

- *Take Charge Product Management* Toolkit
- Product Management Essentials
- Multi-Year Product Strategy (and Planning)
- Clarifying Roles and Handoffs
- The Project Survival Toolkit
- The Project Management Essentials Toolkit

Made in the USA
Lexington, KY
21 September 2017